SOCCER

6

SOCCER

JOHN MOYNIHAN

Contents

THOMAS Y. CROWELL COMPANY
New York/Established 1834

7

Gerd Müller of West Germany rises
high in a 1970 World Cup match

Acknowledgements

The publishers are grateful to the following for
supplying illustrations:

Radio Times Hulton Picture Library 2–3, 16–17,
22–23, 24, 27, 39, 61, 84, 94–95; Syndication
International 5, 6–7, 8–9, 10, 13, 30, 41, 46, 48,
51, 55, 71, 73, 74, 77, 78, 81, 87; Associated
Press 14–15, 28, 30, 35, 55, 62, 64, 65, 66, 68,
70, 75, 78; Mansell Collection 19, 20; Central
Press Photos 30, 54, 77, 87; London Photo
Agency 33; Mirrorpic 36; Popperfoto 46;
Colorsport 88

Front endpapers: West Ham supporters arrive
for the West Ham vs. Bolton Wanderers Cup
Final at Wembley April 1923. Frontispiece: A
familiar Brazilian scene—Pele and Tostao
celebrate scores in a 1970 World Cup match in
Mexico. Title pages: Mick Jones of Leeds
trying a haphazard bicycle kick vs. Manchester
United—not the Anglo-Saxon style. Back
endpapers: The Corinthian team in training in
January 1923.

Library of Congress Catalog Card No: 74-139-08

Design by Steve Pomfret

Illustration research by Penny Brown

Drawings by Paul Thomas

First published 1974, by
Macmillan London Limited
London and Basingstoke
Associated companies in New York, Toronto,
Dublin, Melbourne, Johannesburg and Delhi

Phototypeset by Oliver Burridge Filmsetting Limited,
Crawley, Sussex
Printed in Great Britain by Shenval Press Limited,
Harlow, Essex

ISBN 0-690-00712-4

9

1 WORLD WATCHING AND PLAYING

Soccer is the greatest spectator sport in the world. An estimated television audience of one and a half billion people watched the 1974 World Cup finals in West Germany as sixteen finalists including the host country, Brazil (the 1970 holders), Italy, Scotland and Holland, booted a football around in quest of soccer's most coveted prize. The immense spread of the game since the Second World War was emphasized by the number of nations who took part in the qualifying games leading up to the finals: nearly a hundred from lands as far apart as Iceland and South Korea.

Among the leading nations who failed to reach the finals were England, who mothered the modern game during the last half of the nineteenth century, Hungary and Portugal. For those countries left behind, there was only bitter disappointment, a loss of pride and the long wait to the next World Cup finals in Argentina in 1978: for the successful qualifiers invited to play in nine selected stadiums in West Germany, there was almost a feeling of taking part in a religious rather than sporting festival. For the average man living in the average, universal town, modern soccer has become a kind of stimulant, a regular solace from the greyness of living.

Thousands of spectators—coffee workers from Brazil, waiters from Milan, dockers from the Clyde, ranchers from the Argentine and farmers from Australia—converged on the German venues, Berlin, Hamburg, Dusseldorf and Munich, to cheer and boo

modern football heroes like Gerd Müller (West Germany) and
Luigi Riva (Italy). Throughout three weeks of competition involving
thirty-eight games, the faces of the fans took on a flushed glow of
expectancy; defeat turned their cheeks grey—the cup syndrome
dominated their lives to such an extent that their only reminder of
the outside world was the odd scribbled postcard from home.
Before the games, they gathered in large, anxious groups dis-
cussing the prospects. A lost ticket brought threats close to
suicide. On winning nights, they massed together bellowing out
their national songs in beer halls in celebration.

Such patriotism proved once again how contagious an attraction the game of soccer can be. For the winners of the World Cup,
it can bring an extravagance of booty, a resurgence of national
pride, a new following and, for the winning team, a fortune. This
was certainly the case in England after Sir Alf Ramsey's team won
the 1966 World Cup final against West Germany at Wembley: a
vast new section of the nation's population took wing in allegiance
to their team and the game itself. They did so chiefly through what
they had seen on television, the excitement of the home team
winning, the joy of seeing a toothless Nobby Stiles knocking down
Eusebio with a crisp tackle, the thrill of Bobby Charlton and Geoff
Hurst shooting into the enemy's net. As any top manager will
confirm, there is nothing like success in soccer. By contrast, since
England's two subsequent failures in the World Cup, there has
been a great deal of written and oral disenchantment directed not
only against the English national team but soccer in general.

Certainly the game at home has lost its appeal for many people,
chiefly because of a marked decline in playing skills since 1966,
an upsurge of rough play, dreary and negative tactics, television
mass coverage, spectators' hooliganism and a poor standard of
coaching. But those who therefore brand the game in general as a
declining spectator sport are wide of the mark. Football fans will
continue to watch football as long as they feel they are going to be
entertained: this was proved after England's dismissal by Poland
in the 1973 World Cup qualifying match at Wembley. In England's
next match, a friendly against Italy at the same stadium, the
attendance was over 80,000.

The fascination of playing and watching soccer never ceases
to spread around the globe. In West Germany league attendance
rose sharply before the 1974 World Cup, despite the rival attraction of television. And there are nearly 95,000 registered West
German teams, ranging from top-class teams to schoolboy
combinations. In Russia, over four million players are registered
and they have nearly 200,000 pitches to play on. In France, a
comparatively humble nation in terms of international football,
there are nearly a million registered footballers from professional
to amateur levels. Italy has 116 teams in their three major leagues
and 3,000 smaller clubs. The top Italian league games in Milan

and Turin attract regular gates of about 80,000, and whipped on by a fanatical sporting press, who encourage from their millions of readers an almost religious allegiance to the team's cause, wealthy industrial-sponsored clubs, like Milan, Inter-Milan and Juventus, live the lives of aristocrats. So also in Spain, where wealthy teams such as Barcelona and Real Madrid attract similarly high attendances at their home games. And, like the Italians, they can afford to pay out vast sums on signing players. In the summer of 1973 Barcelona paid the Dutch champions, Ajax of Amsterdam, an astounding £900,000 for their leading player Johan Cruyff. Cruyff took a large lump of that sum for himself, but his regular presence in the Barcelona side quickly repaid the fee through the sales of high-priced tickets.

When Brazil won the World Cup in Mexico in 1970 they were followed by a multitude of colourful, chanting supporters, and any neutral spectator who attended the final, in which they beat Italy at the Aztec Stadium, must have been overwhelmed and temporarily deafened by the ecstatic pleasure the Brazilian congregation uninhibitedly displayed that morning. When Pele scored their opening goal, the rejoicing, the green and yellow banner-waving, the blast of firecrackers seemed to echo all the way back to Rio de Janeiro and those yellow beaches where Pele's forerunners began to kick a ball around at the start of the century.

Pele, the folk hero, once said: 'I came from nothing.' It was to football that he owed everything, his rise from an impoverished shanty existence to the life of a millionaire had everything to do with the round ball and a legion of fans from a country renowned for its football and coffee. But the average Brazilian puts soccer before the beans.

No nation can match the fervour soccer creates in Brazil. Defeat can bring a period of national mourning as happened in 1950, when the home country were beaten in the World Cup final by Uruguay in Rio de Janeiro. There was even the odd suicide to record the moment of horror when Uruguay scored the winning goal. The same fanaticism exists in other South American countries, especially Argentina, Peru and Uruguay, but the emphasis on unruly behaviour often engulfs the passion. In Argentina, the average fan watches the game from wire fences and moats and the police often dampen his ardour with tear gas.

In South America violence stems generally from a fear of defeat and the consequent loss of prestige. Europe has also had its bad cases of spectators running riot: the Glasgow Rangers fans who went berserk in Barcelona after a European Cup Winners' Cup Final against Moscow Dynamo in 1971 were brazen examples. And when Austria played Hungary in a World Cup match the Austrian fans afterwards went round Budapest trying hard to wreck the city. England has also had its football hooliganism of late, but the violent behaviour has chiefly been reserved for local

Left: In the rough and tumble of American football, a Detroit Lion takes to the air. Centre: Phil Woosman (left) signs on as Manager-Coach of Atlanta, a team in the new North American Professional Soccer League. Right: In the 1971 Missouri Amateur Cup Soccer Championship, a player bluntly makes his point. In fact the finger missed the eye

league games, a war between rival gangs often waged through self-indulgent boredom and lack of other social facilities, rather than loyalties inspired by the game itself.

But the typical fan is an average, sober man looking for his Saturday or Sunday afternoon's fun at the stadium. A football match brings out a most remarkable change in the temperament of a doctor, builder, gasman, baker and candlestickmaker. Through the week they are all possibly shy, inoffensive men; at the big match they can suddenly turn into raving, rambling, verbal lunatics, yelling instructions and barracking poor unfortunates down there on the pitch. It is all proof of what has been called 'soccer madness'.

Europe and South America represent the main blocks of global soccer and will probably remain so for the next two generations, despite soccer's increased popularity in Africa and certain parts of Asia, where China and Japan have both revived their interest. There are signs of a new uplift in the United States despite the initial failure to launch a National Professional Soccer League in the mid-sixties.

Soccer in the United States is popular in colleges and schools. Although big pro all-American football, baseball and basketball continue to be the dominant national sports, especially on the main television networks, certain areas of the country are going over to soccer as a game both to play and watch. And a unit from a touring side like the Brazilian team Santos can really pack a stadium in New York. In a recent North American Soccer League match in Dallas, Texas, between the local team and the Philadelphia Atoms, the attendance was 18,824—a turnout to delight

the league commissioner Phil Woosnam. Woosnam, a former Welsh international and West Ham player, went to America to help launch the professional league. Early on he suffered several disappointments, but the fact that eighteen thousand people in Texas wanted to leave their homes to watch a game of soccer is proof that something is stirring. Another encouraging sign is the increase of players in Dallas alone. In 1967, there were eleven amateur clubs in and around the city. A recent census in 1973 showed that 25,000 to 30,000 people had taken up playing the game and that there were 1,170 teams.

A strong North American league must be an asset for soccer in general and could bring a new financial stimulus, through television, to a game which has lately lost too many spectators and followers to be healthy. In the same way, the formation of a European league operating between fifteen, say, top clubs including Red Star (Yugoslavia), Bayern Munich (West Germany), Dynamo Dresden (East Germany), Juventus, A. C. Milan and Inter-Milan (Italy), Barcelona and Real Madrid (Spain), Ajax of Amsterdam, Rangers and Celtic (Scotland), and Leeds and Chelsea (England) could bring to the club game fresh attraction and glamour.

As colour television multiplies round the world, so too does a new brand of soccer television spectactors. What they want to watch generally is far more sophisticated than their brothers on the terraces or up in the stands find so fulfilling. The television networks may bring about a global revolution in the organization and practice of the game.

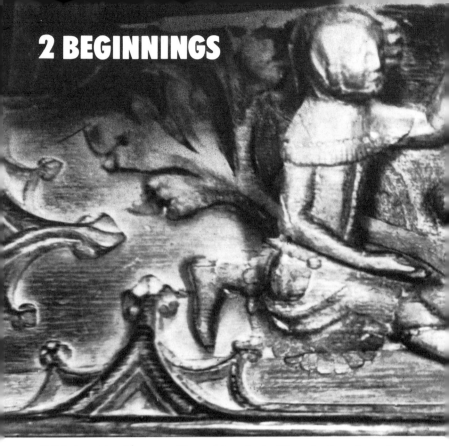

2 BEGINNINGS

If this book had been written at the start of the nineteenth century, the writer would have taken a considerably more pessimistic view of the power and magic of the game. One has only to refer to Joseph Strutt's book *The Sports and Pastimes of the People of England* to see how low the author—a devoted follower of cricket —regarded football as a rural and social recreation. But it would not be long before football began to prosper in the English public schools and be split into two camps, by courtesy of a certain William Webb Ellis, who picked up the ball one afternoon at Rugby in 1823 and had the cheek to run with it.

But that was after Strutt wrote his book and, in 1801, he could only solemnly comment that 'football was formerly much in vogue among the common people of England, though of late years it seems to have fallen into disrepute, and is but little practised . . .' How much the scene has changed over 170 years can be noted from a train window passing a team-massed Stockport recreation ground on a Sunday afternoon, or from a jet plane coming into land at Heathrow over an oily green patchwork covered by a multitude of wiggling human ants playing soccer.

Strutt's conception of the early pioneering mood of Association Football may have been put over without much love or enthusiasm, but in reading the following paragraph there does not seem much difference between what players did then and what they do now:

'When a match at football is made, two parties, each
containing an equal number of competitors, take the
field, and stand between the goals, placed at the
distance of eighty or an hundred yards the one from
the other. The goal is usually made with two sticks
driven into the ground, about two or three feet apart.
The ball, which is commonly made of a blown
bladder, and cased with leather, is delivered in the
midst of the ground, and the object of each party is
to drive it through the goal of their antagonists, which
being achieved the game is won. The abilities of the
performers are best displayed in attacking and
defending the goals; and hence the pastime was
frequently called a goal at foot-ball than a game of
football. When the exercise becomes exceedingly
violent, the players kick each other's shins without
the least ceremony, and some of them are over-
thrown at the hazard of their limbs.'

The goals have widened since then but certainly there has not
been much change in the earthier side of the game: shin kicking
remains commonplace, limbs are still ready to lash out: the

17

blown, inflated white footballs skim the chins of bellowing giants
muttering oaths.

Strutt's researches into the history of football do not go back
much beyond the reign of Edward III when 'in 1349, it was pro-
hibited by a public edict; not, perhaps, from any objection to the
sport in itself, but because it co-operated, with other favourite
amusements, to impede the progress of archery.' But certainly
the ancestry of the game can now be traced back centuries before,
to 206 BC, when it was played in China during the Han Dynasty
under the name of *Tsu Chu.*

An historian of the period described it in his records as '*Tsu*
must kick. *Chu* is the stuffed leather ball.' There was always a
special football match played on the emperor's birthday with two
teams competing on a pitch alongside the royal pavilion. The
goals consisted of two bamboo posts 30 foot high, with two silk
goal nets attached to the bases. The players were required to
kick the horsehair football towards each other's goal net in front
of the grinning emperor and his entourage of nobles and foreign
visitors.

Tsu Chu had a similar social standing at the Chinese court as
polo does with modern royalty—the emperor Ch'eng Ti was an
accomplished player himself. His ministers complained that such
exertions were undignified for an emperor, while his empress
implored him to take up tiddlywinks. But Ch'eng Ti persisted with
the game, as did a subsequent emperor, who was so incensed by
a member of his court criticizing *Tsu Chu* that he had the unfortu-
nate executed.

Tsu Chu match winners were always highly rewarded by the
emperor after beating their opponents by kicking more goals into
a net a yard wide. They were given various food and wine deli-
cacies while the other team was either beheaded or flogged,
depending on the mood of the emperor. A Chinese poet of the
period Li-Yu (50–130 AD) supplied the following ode to the game:

> *A round ball and an oblong space, with*
> *two teams standing opposed.*
> *The ball flies across like the moon at*
> *the full.*
> *Captains are appointed and take their*
> *places in accordance with regulation*
> *unchanging.*
> *In the game make no allowance for kith and*
> *kin and let not your mind be swayed*
> *by partialities.*
> *Be cool and determined and show not the*
> *slightest irritation when you fail.*

There were other instances of ancient 'footy' in Japan, Greece,

THE country Swaines, at footeball heere are seene,
  Which each gapes after, for to get a blow,
The while some one, away runnes with it cleane,
It meetes another, at the goale below
    Who never stirrd, one catcheth heere a fall,
    And there one's maimd, who never saw the ball.

This worldly wealth, * is tossed too and fro,
At which like Brutes, each striues with might and maine,
To get a kick, by others overthrow,
Heere one's fetch't vp, and there another slaine,
    With eager hast, and then it doth affront
    Some stander by, who never thought vpon't.

Arbiter.

ancient Rome, Brittany and Normandy. The Japanese version over fourteen centuries ago was a decorative pastime, far less hostile than the Chinese version. Their game was called *Kemari* and consisted of genteel passing between players on a pitch surrounded by cherry and maple trees. The Japanese tend to be very polite until they are really aroused, but there are no instances in the records of any violence in this game. The Greeks invented a game called *harpaston* played with a ball full of sand, a game similar to the *harpastium* the Romans are said to have introduced to the ancient Britons.

The Bretons and the Normans had their own individual game named *soule* which they probably introduced to Britain when William the Conqueror crossed the Channel in 1066. Here the interesting part of the game was distance: it didn't matter how far the competitors ran with the ball because there were no touch-lines. Which meant the combatants could gallop away for miles with a wooden or leather object at their feet, and the opposition might take a few hours to catch up with them and kick the ball back to the original starting point.

From these early scrambles came more cultural codes such as the Florentine game of *calcio* of medieval times. This was a game of enormous pomp and courtly splendour played in the Piazza della Signorina in Florence in front of a crowd of foreign diplomats, dukes, princes and their reigning mistresses. Betting was rife. Six umpires officiated at the match played on a pitch 400 feet by 500 feet in area. Twenty-seven players in sumptuous costumes made up each side; they were allowed to use their hands as well as their feet, so *calcio* in its embryonic form must have been one of the earliest prototypes of rugby. But the dribbling skills of the Florentines were certainly an early hint of what the modern masters from Milan, Turin, and Florence now achieve. The contests were held, and still are, much to the joy of American tourists, on festival days.

Following Roman and Breton influences, football in medieval England turned into rough and ready scrummages between neighbouring towns, villages and manors. Serf often kicked hogs' heads around and, on feast days like Shrove Tuesday, especially in Chester, there were wild confrontations involving every available fit man in the area. In Chester the shoemakers took on the drapers, a good way to let off steam. Although successive monarchs, including Edward II, Edward III and Henry IV tended to frown on the proceedings as being undignified, football still remained popular enough among the people to inspire such early poems as:

> *And nowe in the winter, when men kill the*
> *fat swine,*
> *They get the bladder and blow it great and thin,*
> *With many beans and person put within:*
> *It ratleth, soundeth, and shineth clere and*
> *fayre,*
> *While it is throwen and caste up in the ayre,*
> *Each one contendeth and hath a great delite*
> *With foote and with hands the bladder for to*
> *smite;*
> *If it fall to grounde, they lifte it up agayne,*
> *But this waye to labour they count it no payne.*

James I also found football distasteful and tried once again to bar it from the land with the order: 'From this court I debarre all rough and violent exercises, as the foot-ball, meeter for lameing than making able the users thereof.' His grandson, Charles II, was one of the first monarchs in England to really encourage the sport and once watched a match played in his own royal grounds on a pitch similar in size to a pitch of today.

His interest in the game was aroused by Count Albemarle, who had returned from Italy in 1681 puffing and wheezing with pleasure about a game of *calcio* he had seen in Florence. The result was a challenge match between a team put out by the merry monarch and the Count. It ended in an away win for Albemarle and cost Charles ten gold coins. But he enjoyed the match so much that he ruled that football was indeed a game fit for the people, and the royal ban was cancelled.

Football continued to flourish in certain urban districts in Georgian times with players rattling a ball around narrow, darkened streets in clogs. There were instances of games played by hoards of rough youths in the Strand in London in the middle of the eighteenth century—but in general, football was still far from organized. There are also records of a match played in 1793 between Norton and Sheffield when six players from Norton, wearing green, took on six from Sheffield in red. The match lasted three days and spiritedly ended in a battle of fists in which several players were nearly killed.

A game of football at Rugby School in 1845

The real beginnings of what we term the modern game came after the Napoleonic Wars. British public schools, including Westminster, Charterhouse, Winchester, Eton and Harrow, evolved their own codes of football, while universities, notably Cambridge, also took up the game. The Cambridge Rules were conceived in 1848, and gradually the game blossomed. Early dribbling with a round ball contrasted with the handling game started by Dr Arnold's Rugby School and made famous in *Tom Brown's Schooldays.* The first crossbars were introduced in 1865, though still only as a piece of string connecting two posts. Two years later offside was brought in and a little later, the two teams were only allowed to use one goalkeeper each. The wooden crossbar was introduced in 1874 and in 1881 referees assumed the role of the set of umpires.

In the more elementary years between 1830 and 1840, soccer emerged as a game for splendid young gentlemen rather than a game fit for unruly mobsters. Schools like Westminster and Charterhouse pioneered the dribbling game, a delicate form of play compared with all the hacking and in-fighting that had gone before. It seemed that public school soccer, along with the handling code of other schools, was the perfect means to exercise hearty, privileged youth brought together in an otherwise

rigorous Victorian atmosphere, where a high standard of religious morality was strictly observed in the shadow of the birch. But out on the football field, it was permissible to sacrifice every painful muscle in favour of the muddy cause.

But during the 1860s, the public schoolboys began to lose ground to working-class teams up north—the founding of the Sheffield Club in 1855 made it the oldest club in the business and was reputed to be inspired by some visiting Harrovians who visited the poor district as missionaries. The oldest Football League club to emerge was Notts County, launched in 1862, three years before their neighbours Nottingham Forest. The balance of power in soccer was moving to the industrial cities but it was at a London public house, the Freemason's Tavern in Great Queen Street, one evening in December 1863 that one of the most important events in the history of soccer occurred.

On that gaslit night, the Football Association was formed—the first body in the world to control soccer as a national concern. One or two committee members at the meeting, including F. W. Campbell of the Blackheath Club, argued about the adoption of the Cambridge Rules. It led to a split. Campbell and his rebels went their 'handling' way: eight years later the Rugby Union was formed.

SMYTH.

One of the first internationals between England and Scotland: sketches drawn at the International Football Match at Glasgow taken from the *Graphic* newspaper of 14 December 1872

SKETCHES AT THE INTERNATIONAL FOOTBALL MATCH, GLASGOW

Thus Association Football or soccer was officially born. C. W. Alcock, an old Harrovian, took over as secretary of the Football Association and the game began to prosper for a brief period in an entirely amateur game. Alcock inspired the launching of the F.A. Cup competition with the words: 'It is desirable that a Challenge Cup should be established in connection with the Association, for which all clubs belonging to the Association should be invited to compete.'

The first F.A. Cup Final took place at Kennington Oval in 1872 when the famous Wanderers beat the Royal Engineers 1—0 in front of 2,000 people. The Wanderers won the trophy again a year later at the same ground, beating Oxford University 2—0. The attendance rose by thousands. By 1901, when Tottenham and Sheffield United drew in a Cup Final at Crystal Palace, the attendance was 110,820. Over the years, the lure of the Cup had become phenomenal. The original F.A. Cup was bought for £20 from the jewellers Martin, Hall and Co. In 1900 it was stolen from a shop window in Birmingham and replaced by the present trophy.

The later half of the nineteenth century saw the rise of the first great professional clubs like Preston North End (the first team to win the Football League championship and the F.A. Cup in the same season) Aston Villa, Blackburn Rovers and Newcastle United. C. W. Alcock was instrumental in legalizing professionalism, after a period of undercover payments between clubs and their players. In 1885, Alcock and the Football Association ordained a hitherto highly frowned on subject and the first players to register as professionals were two Scotsmen, Suter and Love, who played for Darwen in Lancashire. Previously clubs like Preston had supported their star players by giving them financial perks and part-time jobs in the town: now they could pay them a normal wage without resorting to what the gentlemen amateurs regarded as unethical behaviour.

The first Scottish club, Queen's Park, was formed in 1867 but the Scottish Football Association did not appear until 1873, ten years after the Football Association. This is not to say the game had not taken a firm hold over the border, especially in the slum areas of Glasgow. Scottish players, as they do now, went south to join the prosperous English teams but it was inevitable that the two countries would eventually meet in an international match. The first game took place in Glasgow in 1872 and no goals were scored that day. It started a regular run of international matches between Scotland and England; in some of the early games the Scots, by introducing a clever passing brand of football, outmatched the English who concentrated on dribbling. The Scots cut them apart.

The 1880s brought a new maturity to football. The Football League was founded in England in 1888 consisting of the main clubs of the time who would compete for an annual trophy, separate from the F.A. Cup. The Football Association and the Football League have often remained as much apart as organizations as Paris and London as cities, and still remain proudly responsible for their own competitions. At times an increased liaison between them might have benefited the English game in general.

The first Football League clubs were Accrington, Aston Villa, Blackburn Rovers, Bolton Wanderers, Burnley, Derby County, Everton, Notts County, Preston North End, Stoke City, West Bromwich Albion and Wolverhampton Wanderers. Of the twelve, only Accrington failed to survive the years and they did not drop out until 1962, chiefly because of financial troubles under the name of Accrington Stanley. Preston won the first League Championship. The number of League clubs now totals ninety-two.

It was during this period when the Victorians were busily building up a large Empire overseas that the game began to spread abroad to other countries. The teachers and the messengers were British sailors, missionaries, engineers and miners who kicked a football around in foreign lands. In Spain, the game was at first looked on as a threat to bull-fighting but later was merrily taken up by youths in Madrid. In South America, the game spread from the port areas along the River Plate where British ships put in while in Brazil; the negro population took up football, nursing it with their peculiar, devastating skills on beaches and back areas because they were barred from playing the game on official football grounds.

One of the main pioneers of football in the Argentine was Alexander Watt, a Cambridge University player who inspired the Alumni Club there. When a team of students from the National College took part in a game he had organized they were arrested by the police for wearing short pants. In Germany, a British footballer practising heading by nodding the ball against a wall was arrested by an innocent local policeman thinking the man was trying to commit suicide. Those were early days, and odd stories like that abounded because foreigners had never seen this strange game played with a leather ball before. But, gradually, the magic of the game was officially recognized: France, Spain, Switzerland and Belgium were among the first European teams to play soccer, and England's first international match abroad took place on 6 June 1908 against Austria: England beat them 6—1. The new boys still had a lot to learn.

The creation of an international football union was inspired by a Dutch banker called C. Hirschmann in 1902 but when the idea was put forward to the English Football Association, the matter was treated in London as a frivolous idea. So when F.I.F.A. (the Federation of International Football Associations) was formed two

The Roaring Twenties: crowds invade
Wembley Stadium for the first Cup
Final held there in 1923 between West
Ham and Bolton Wanderers

years later, England were not among the original nations enrolled. The first seven countries were France, Belgium, Holland, Switzerland, Spain, Denmark and Sweden. The membership of F.I.F.A. in the 1970s is over 100, swelled recently by a host of African countries. England grudgingly enrolled in 1906 but pulled out in the twenties on a question of amateurism. It was not until 1946 that England, with Wales, Scotland and Northern Ireland, rejoined F.I.F.A. having missed competing in all the initial World Cup competitions held before the outbreak of war in 1939. The World Cup had been the idea of a Frenchman, Jules Rimet, and the first competition held in 1930 in Uruguay was won by the host nation.

The Olympic Games continued to be the main football competition up to the thirties and when Great Britain put out a team in London in 1908, they won the final by beating Denmark 2—0. The old Olympian amateur spirit continued to exist in English international teams right into the twenties. Some foreign opposition was still very weak and usually the amateurs sent out to play them representing England, teams like the enthusiastic Middlesex Wanderers and the famous Corinthians, were quite capable of beating another country's first team handsomely.

But the move towards professionalism gathered momentum

after the First World War, and the standard of foreign opposition began to improve. England were beaten for the first time by a foreign team on foreign soil when Spain won 4—3. The challenge was strengthening, yet some English football administrators were ludicrously slow in heeding, let alone rating it. Meanwhile, English and Scottish soccer were producing great club teams. In England, Huddersfield became a fine postwar team winning three successive League championships in the 1920s.

Arsenal was another club to emerge as a considerable force in the twenties and thirties. Their manager and inspiration was Herbert Chapman who had previously run Huddersfield during their prime. Chapman built the North London team around Charlie Buchan, a natural, constructive centre forward, and when the offside law was changed, invented the 'stopper' centre forward to counteract the opposition's raiding centre forwards. One of Chapman's most memorable moments in a career in which he emerged as one of the most inspired managers in history—Sir Matt Busby and Jock Stein are two others—was the 1930 Cup Final when Arsenal met Huddersfield and won by 2—0.

The venue for F.A. Cup Finals became the property of Wembley Stadium in 1923 when it opened to coincide with the Empire Exhibition. A crowd of almost 150,000 invaded the stadium that day, many massing around the playing area for the match between

Bolton and West Ham. George V stood silently in the Royal Box facing a sea of claustrophobic subjects, trying to calm with his royal presence what was thought might turn into a hideous disaster. But although the monarch tried his best, a policeman on a white horse actually did his job more effectively through the friendly bumps of his nag's rump. The two teams managed a start, Bolton scored a quick goal and then added another in the second half.

Wembley Cup Finals subsequently became all-ticket occasions limited to 100,000 spectators. There were some historic matches up to the Second World War. In 1927, Cardiff City beat Arsenal by 1—0: a fluke goal which slipped under the Arsenal goalkeeper Lewis's body. It was the first and only time the F.A. Cup has gone outside England.

In 1932, Arsenal lost 2—1 to Newcastle United, a match still renowned for the controversy caused by the second goal scored by the 'Magpies', as Newcastle were known. Old newsreels still show the ball was over the goal line when the Newcastle winger centred for Richardson to head into the net.

Apart from Wembley Stadium, the shape and size of British stadiums altered considerably with the turn of the century. Soccer as a massed attraction, particularly in Scotland, caused the building of such stadiums in Glasgow as Ibrox Park—home of Glasgow Rangers—and Hampden Park. The great rivalry between the Protestant-orientated Rangers and Glasgow Celtic, the Catholics, or 'Papists' as the Rangers fans often mockingly named them, drew crowds of 100,000. And when Scotland met England in 1937, the attendance at Hampden Park was 149,547, a record which is unlikely ever to be beaten. Such attendances were only twice instrumental in major crowd disasters in Scotland and once in England—a mercifully low figure considering the poor safety standards at some grounds.

Football grounds built earlier in the century were largely designed to accommodate large masses of people without shelter. The covered stands were monopolized by wealthier people who could afford the luxury of sitting down. The progressive Arsenal Football Club opened a new luxurious stadium at Highbury after the First World War with far more covered accommodation, and a clock at one end, and it became renowned as one of the finest grounds in the world. But after the Second World War, older, more antiquated grounds, some badly bombed, had to cope again with a massive new enthusiasm for watching soccer. Crowds of up to 80,000 were commonplace in the middle forties and when the Russian team Moscow Dynamo played Chelsea at Stamford Bridge in 1945, nearly 90,000 people were there to see the game. A good ten thousand broke into the ground after the gates had been shut, and sat on the roof of the main stand and spilled out round the pitch. The match was drawn 3—3.

Now, happily, across the world, new stadiums are being built with few open areas. Every spectator will soon be able to watch in comparative comfort. And with the majority of fans seated, we must hope clubs will have seen the last of their resident hooligans. The evidence, especially in the United States, is that sports fans do not normally fight or riot when they are sitting down.

Football throughout Europe generally prospered in the early years after the Second World War. The enormous attendances were proof of a huge new enthusiasm for the game after the grind of the war years; on 17 January 1948 a crowd of 82,950 watched Manchester United play Arsenal on the Maine Road ground, loaned by Manchester City because Old Trafford was still being rebuilt after war damage. This set up a record for an English league game that has yet to be beaten and will probably never be. The Scots had their fanatics, too, and when Rangers and Hibernian were matched in a Scottish Cup semi-final at Hampden Park in March 1948, 143,570 souls turned up to watch.

When England, Scotland, Northern Ireland and Wales rejoined F.I.F.A. after the war a celebration match in 1947 between Great Britain and the Rest of Europe was held at Hampden Park. The British side, consisting of five Englishmen, three Scotsmen, two Welshmen and one Northern Ireland representative, trounced the Rest 6—1, Mannion and Lawton each scoring two goals for Great Britain. In 1953, when England met the Rest of Europe in a match to celebrate the ninetieth anniversary of the Football Association, they were fortunate to get a 4—4 draw, Alf Ramsey having equalized with a penalty near the end.

In the period from 1947 to 1953, England's superiority in international matches began to decline, although at first there was no sign of any sudden deterioration. To begin with, England had some magnificent victories and they outmatched and outplayed some difficult opposition. They had some highly talented players: Swift in goal, the young Billy Wright of Wolves captaining the side at right half (he went on to win 105 caps, the first England player ever to reach, let alone pass, a century), Stanley Matthews, the 'wizard of dribble', on the right wing, Neil Franklin, master of the short pass at centre half, Wilf Mannion, a golden craftsman at inside left, Tommy Lawton, a deadly centre forward and vitriolic in the air, Stan Mortensen, always going for goal like a greased piston engine, and Tom Finney on the left wing, elusive and blessed with all-round skills—many say made him England's greatest footballer in history. No wonder teams suffered, including Italy by 4 clear goals, Portugal by 10 and the Olympic champions, Sweden, by 4—2.

But when the team began to break up and loss of form and injury hampered the England selectors, their own debatable choices and reluctance to play Matthews and Finney in the same side was sometimes difficult to fathom. The result was failure in

the 1950 World Cup in Brazil when the England side were beaten
by a near-novice team from the United States. England continued
to be managed by the academic Walter Winterbottom into the
early 1960s, when he was replaced by Alf Ramsey; the results in
the next three World Cups in 1954, 1958 and 1962 were equally
disappointing.

It was on a misty afternoon in the autumn of 1953 that English
football as a dominant power was scuttled at Wembley by a
massively superior Hungarian side (3—6). It led to a full-scale
inquiry into the wrongs of English football and the Football
Association under their secretary Sir Stanley Rous (now president
of F.I.F.A.) set up a number of technical committees to explore the
situation. Like all committees of this nature the tortoise moved
slowly and a dozen more years went by before England won the
World Cup on their own soil at Wembley, beating West Germany
4—2 after extra time. That much hailed result would prove to be
the blinking beacon between the Hungarian disaster and Poland's
elimination of England in the World Cup qualifying group in
October, 1973. Once again the pressure is on to see what ails
English football.

In the fifties, a first move was to change the image of the
English footballer from a solid, heavy-booted warrior in baggy
shorts and heavy socks into something akin to their lighter,
snappier continental rivals. Sir Matt Busby created his famous, all-
conquering Manchester United 'Babes' whose youth, enthusiasm
and skills enraptured the whole nation. They were one of the first
teams to launch the new streamlined image into English football
both in tactics and turn-out, and when sixteen of their members
were killed in the Munich air crash in 1958 including the legendary
England half-back, Duncan Edwards, Manchester went downhill,
cloaked in mourning. Sir Matt Busby barely survived the crash to
build up another great Manchester United side which became the
first, and so far, only English team to win the European Cup
against Benfica in 1968.

English football in the fifties and early sixties may not have
produced many sparks from the national team but it did produce
some distinguished club teams as well as managers. Apart from
Sir Matt and his pastmasters Manchester United, Tottenham
Hotspur blossomed twice with superb combinations. In the early
fifties, their push-and-run side under Arthur Rowe could be
positively symphonic; then came the great side of a decade later
managed by Bill Nicholson and captained by Danny Blanchflower. This team became the first in the twentieth century to win
the Football League championship and the F.A. Cup in the same
season. Arsenal repeated the process in 1971.

Another fine side was the Wolverhampton Wanderers team
captained by Billy Wright and managed by Stan Cullis. Their use
of long passes and two speedy wingers, Hancocks and Mullen,

John Charles, Wales's greatest player,
who had a distinguished career with
Juventus

overcame such sides as the formidable Honved from Hungary in the mid-fifties.

When improved air travel inspired new international competitions at leading club level—the European Cup, the European Cup Winners' Cup and the U.E.F.A. Cup—it was Real Madrid who at first became the dominating force. With great players like di Stefano and Puskas in the side, they won the first five European Cup competitions. Their exuberance and almost telepathic teamwork in their clinically all-white strip became a regular joy for the rapidly expanding European television audience.

After England won the World Cup in 1966, Alf Ramsey became Sir Alf and the game took on a new lease of life all over the United Kingdom. New sections of the populace were enticed into watching the game, not to mention a large segment of the show business advertizing clan. Celtic became the first British team to win the European Cup by beating Inter-Milan 2—1, and when Manchester United followed suit a year later, our football was sitting, very temporarily, on a previously unscaled ridge of success. But after the World Cup in Mexico things began to go depressingly wrong.

England had been rather unlucky to be eliminated in their quarter-final match against West Germany in Leon, Mexico. They were leading 2—0 but finally lost 3—2 in extra time partly due to goalkeeping errors by Bonetti of Chelsea, who had come in at the last moment in place of the outstanding Banks, suddenly crippled by a stomach bug. The wonderful Brazilians eventually won the final beating Italy and were allowed to keep the Jules Rimet trophy having won it three times, in 1958, 1962 and 1970.

In 1973, England were later beaten in the quarter finals of the European Nations Cup by West Germany and criticism of Sir Alf Ramsey's defensive tactics, undue caution and lack of creative style in the side rose from a murmur into a shout. The side were expected to qualify for the World Cup finals in 1974 but having lost loyal and talented players like Banks, Geoff Hurst, Jack Charlton and Bobby Charlton, they first went down to Poland by 2—0 at Katowice in the summer of 1973 and later in a thrilling group return at Wembley could only draw 1—1. Poland qualified because England had only been able to draw with the other member of their group, Wales, earlier in the year. Postmortems naturally sizzled unabated: in 1974, Sir Alf was deposed as England's team manager. A return to wing-play was called for in the tradition of Stanley Matthews and Tom Finney in combination with the ball-playing skills of Wilf Mannion. Less physical intervention, more creation in attack. But whatever progress England makes in the future, a long road stretches ahead to the 1978 World Cup finals in the Argentine. A happy consolation was the qualification of Scotland for the 1974 World Cup finals. Their national team had been in the backwoods for too long and had not been seen in any previous finals since 1958.

3 THE SOCCER PROFESSIONAL

In the fifties a professional footballer's basic salary in England averaged £12 a week. But since the abolition of the maximum wage in 1961 when Johnny Haynes of Fulham became the first £100 a week player, the status of the game has been so upgraded that its more illustrious performers can afford to take on an expensive lifestyle.

It took a long time coming. After professionalism was made legal by the Football Association back in 1885, the pay packets of players ranged from 25 new pence to 50 new pence. When the Football League took over control of the players' welfare from the Football Association before the First World War, the maximum wage had risen to £4. Wages climbed slowly for footballers despite the enormous popularity of the game and by 1961, the maximum wage was still only a pathetic £20 a week.

Players like John Charles, Denis Law, Gerry Hitchens and Jimmy Greaves countered this by going off to Italy and earning far larger salaries. Charles had a particularly long, lucrative and happy stay with Juventus of Turin, in contrast to Greaves who played but briefly with Inter-Milan. Charles and company were not the first British players to go abroad in search of higher salaries. Several Chelsea players went to France before the out-

A typical salmon leap by Denis Law of
Manchester United against Chelsea.
The bemused goalkeeper is Bonetti of
Chelsea

break of the Second World War but found themselves being treated as second-class citizens.

England centre half Neil Franklin and his Stoke team mate George Mountford ran off to Bogotá to join the Santa Fé Club in 1950. The basic wage then was £12 a week and Franklin sacrificed his place in the England World Cup party for Brazil to earn a higher wage for his family. But things did not work out too well for the two rebels and they came home disillusioned after a few months.

It was Jimmy Hill, a former Fulham player, and now a distinguished soccer commentator with the B.B.C., who led the Professional Football Association into making the Football League do away with the maximum wage in 1961 after a threat of strike action. Two years later, a historic court case took place in the High Court in which Mr Justice Wilberforce ruled that the retain and transfer system was unlawful, being in restraint of a footballer's trade. George Eastham of Newcastle United, assisted by the P.F.A., had brought the case in which the player challenged his club's legal right not to allow him a transfer.

The old transfer system which had virtually made a player a 'slave' of the club he served was thus abolished and a new form of contract, in which he was able to negotiate his own regular contract on a short-term basis, was devised. It made for a much healthier situation, although the clubs themselves were protected in the sense that a player cannot wander when he just feels like it. But certainly the new financial apparatus brought a new democracy to the professional game.

Since the early 1960s, the working life of a professional footballer has changed radically. Not quite as dramatically as Pele's in Brazil, who emerged from a meagre background to become a millionaire, or the Dutchman, Johan Cruyff's, whose illustrious career with Ajax of Amsterdam was said to have made him a millionaire three times over. But compared with the barren old days, a top professional in the English First Division of twenty-two clubs now lives a life of comparative luxury, with a comfortable suburban house, a large executive car, a newspaper column which he puts his name to but may not write, numerous bonuses, perks and advertising contracts.

His circle of friends, who used to be the cloth-capped mates he bought a round for in the local after the match, now tend to be actors, restaurateurs, and numerous other temporary trendsetters. Some of the players were more adept at settling in with the new deal than others. George Best, the Manchester United and Northern Ireland international, bought himself a luxury home, a Rolls-Royce and a boutique, then simply blew up and summarily left football because of the great pressures. Others, like the more level-headed Bobby Moore (West Ham and Captain of England) and Francis Lee of Manchester City diversified and rose from being shrewd businessmen into tycoons.

4 EQUIPMENT

A raw, inexperienced amateur team will be at a strong psychological advantage in taking the field smartly turned out in a new and colourful strip. The team may not be particularly good but the fact they vaguely look like a group of Bobby Moores, Johan Cruyffs and Eusebios might not only increase their own confidence but also slightly unnerve the opposition at the start. A good turnout is essential: a team in tatters is a ragged team before it starts, a team with an inferiority complex. And it is vital that the manager or coach of a budding team sees that his players turn out wearing the *same* clean strip; same-coloured shorts and stockings are as important as the colour of the shorts although it is not always possible in the lower echelons to conform in the realm of stockings.

The first and most vital thing is to purchase a set of standard shirts. A multi-coloured team may look raffishly endearing to an amused spectator but both teams will find it confusing on the field and a good referee would not allow it.

In England it is possible to order a set of thirteen shirts from large manufacturers at a discount. And sports shops should also give 10 per cent discounts. A collection in the team would make the purchase possible, and here a stern treasurer is necessary in the side.

Boots have changed greatly since the fifties when the Hungarians showed us the value of light, economical strip and light boots. The old heavily protected football boot favoured by British players with bang-in wooden studs gave way to the light 'ballet' type with cutaway heel. These were sold with adjustable, screw-in plastic studs or all weather rubber studs. The early prototypes were far more comfortable than old heavier boots but they often failed to last very long over a muddy winter.

Now the new tougher versions, sold through big German sports combines like Adidas and Puma, usually give a long service and unlimited comfort. If I was to recommend one type, it would be the Adidas 'Austria' with all-weather rubber studs. This is equally practical on wet and frozen grounds and can be used for training throughout the summer. Every player, however, has his own personal favourites and should be left in general to choose his own. A comfortable boot is all important.

It is essential that players keep an eye on their studs. Dangerous studs can cause havoc on a limb and in top-class matches referees always inspect the teams' boots before kick-off. Leather, aluminium, plastic and rubber studs are permissible and should be no less than three-quarters of an inch from the base of the sole. Longish studs are advisable for heavy grounds, shorter ones for a hard surface. On a frozen surface, a rubber-soled training shoe often proves invaluable.

The new boots, however, give less protection to the ankles than their predecessors. But it is possible to buy special shin guards

Times change: Alex James (left), one
of the greatest ball artists of all time,
wears the Arsenal strip of 1930; Bobby
Moore, with 108 caps to his credit, with
the England strip of 1969

which give protection to the ankles and Achilles tendon. Shin guards are mainly important to protect the whole exposed leg below the knee. Many younger players have given up wearing them as a nuisance but soccer is a physical game and a hard tackle can easily cause a nasty bruise or cut. Speaking as a player who was once in receipt of a broken leg, my injury would have been far worse had I not been wearing a shin pad. It took much of the pressure and probably stopped a compound fracture.

Shorts and socks have reduced in size since the days before the war when Alex James would turn out for Arsenal wearing his baggy shorts down to his knees. There is a photograph on a wall at Wembley Stadium of Billy Wright shaking hands with the captain of Argentine: the difference in kit now seems unbelievable. Wright's shorts not only dragged down towards the ground but they were also as wide as a tent. It was amazing that such a skilled and speedy player as he could move at all wearing such formidable pantaloons. The Argentine captain almost wore a bikini in comparison. Shorts and socks in this country are now much lighter, but a player would be advised to wear two pairs of stockings, one to hold his shin pads, the other pair held up with a lace.

Care of your kit is most important, especially of your boots. A pair which has been left to dry out after a wet match without being properly greased will feel as hard as rock the following week and wreak agony on the instep and toes.

There have been inevitable occasions when amateur teams have turned up to play each other without a ball between them. A small club should own at least two quality balls and the odd plastic one for practice—and a special pump for inflating them. The laws of football state that a match ball should be between 27 and 28 inches in circumference; the weight should be between 14 and 16 ounces before the start of play. Remember: an over-inflated ball is horrible to kick, an under-inflated ball feels like wet dough and lopes and swerves around in the air. An ideal ball should have a slight give.

Finally—goalkeepers. Having his own domain to care for, a goalkeeper should make sure he has his own special equipment always at hand. On a sunny day, he will need a cap, not the old rustic type that goalkeepers like Frank Swift used to fancy, but a snappy, close-fitting skiing type. In the old days, goalkeepers sometimes used to lose their caps during a goal-mouth scramble. Goalkeeping jerseys have become mugh lighter with crew necks instead of the old polo-necked type made of heavy wool. A goalkeeper's jersey is usually green: they must always differ in colour from the other shirts on the field. A pair of strong gloves is a vital part of a goalkeeper's equipment. A new type on the market bearing the famous name of Gordon Banks have rubber protectors for the palms and knuckles.

5 BASIC TECHNIQUES

This section is intended essentially as a guide to the basic rudiments of the game for the beginner and *not* as an advanced thesis for the more experienced player. Other authors like Jimmy Hill and F. N. S. Creek, who have played the game at top level, have already published excellent, detailed studies on how to play the game of benefit to both novice and professional (see Further Reading List). So here is not the place to learn how to score a goal with the outside of the heel, but rather how to rise from a young tenderfoot to at least a presentable player by mastering the basic skills. So this section includes a few personal tips for all beginners: they may be of some help during their struggles in face of wind, mud and unfriendly full-backs.

Choosing your position Many players usually choose their regular positions on the pitch early on in life. Goalscorers have a natural ability to put the ball into the net from boyhood and the urge to do so often is not to abate until they retire. Defenders are generally physically tough and strong and enjoy tackling and spoiling, while midfield men tend to have an instinct for constructive tactics and ball play. Sometimes a player may find by accident that he has been playing in the wrong position and has a natural ability as, say, a winger. Top professional players are now encouraged to play an all-round 'total' game, with full-backs overlapping as wingers and defenders coming up as extra forwards.

One most important thing for a novice to remember is that he should try to improve and stretch his own ability and arts to the maximum, whether he be a defender or attacker. A striker may find he has natural talent as scorer but he may have scant knowledge of what to do with the ball between the half-way line and the opposing penalty area. A striker who simply hangs around the opposing goal-mouth with his hands on his hips is a liability to his team mates. So having settled for his favourite position, a young player should extend his range of activity to his fullest.

Playing will certainly become much more enjoyable. The real pleasure of soccer is feeling yourself really part of the proceedings—not simply a piece of useless furniture. It may be a sweet feeling scoring goals, but there are other pleasures to be had: a last minute tackle to save a goal, a particularly elegant cross-field pass over the mud, a dribble past three men, or the accurate corner which finds a colleague waiting to head into the enemy goal. The game can flow with crescendos of action, dying into passages of quiet which dawdle along until the next crescendo. A player should always be on the alert through all a game's moods. A dull ten minutes could lull a team into loss of concentration and lose it a goal. In soccer, it is vital to keep on the alert. And this applies especially to a goalkeeper who has had little to do until suddenly he is faced with a long-range shot; he might fumble the ball through lack of concentration. An alert player is the friend of his team mates, a dozy one becomes their foe.

Ball control One of the most important things for a young player to learn is how he should master the ball rather than letting the ball be the master. A ball quickly brought under control is a ball tamed and ready for exploiting the opposition. Failure to control the ball may mean the opposition gains possession—and that could prove calamitous. So it may take hours and hours of practice kicking a tennis ball against a convenient wall to master simple control like trapping, first-time passing, leading volleying, back-heeling and so on. Some of the great ball players like Charlie Cooke, the Scottish international, learnt their skills by using the wall method for hours and hours on end. Malcolm Allison, the Crystal Palace manager, recently lamented that tennis balls were not being used by boys in practice so much these days: 'I wish I could see more tennis balls in the play-grounds than those of the plastic variety that require little or no true ability to control.'

And Joe Mercer, who had such a distinguished playing career with Everton, Arsenal and England, before becoming a manager, once observed: 'If you can learn to control a small ball with certainty, you'll find later on that the bigger one comes more easily—it's wonderful training for the eye. And the fact of having to play in a confined space—like a back yard—or under other difficulties has its advantages. The best partner I ever had as a boy was one who never spoke to me, a wall . . .'

Once a certain relationship with the ball has been established, a young player should make it work for him by practising overtime. He should take a ball out and try running with it, kicking it for long and short distances, chasing, heading, keeping close control by walking with it and then breaking into a sprint while still trying to keep control.

Some of the great natural players like Tom Finney and Stanley Matthews have been able both to bring the ball under control and to elude the opposition with a sharp burst, almost in one movement. A two-footed player is obviously better equipped to control the ball, so practise controlling the ball with the weaker foot. Another useful training method is to dribble the ball round and round a number of posts, trying to avoid them. Speed up, slow, sprint, slow, push the ball ahead, then keep close control. But don't hit those posts.

Heading Many young players enter soccer thinking that it hurts to head a football. They stand there wincing at the approaching object, brace their frames for the impact, close their eyes and put the top of their craniums forward as a form of shield. In doing so, they will probably be vaguely stunned while the ball bounces away unnavigated. This is all wrong.

Some players never lose their fear of heading the ball and are generally a liability to their team. The way to head a ball is basically fundamental—contact should always be made with the *forehead*, and neck muscles should be arched to provide power

Heading
Head down   Head up

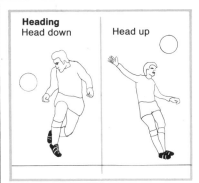

Dribbling Body swerve
and delay tackle

Trapping   Outside   Hollow chest   Cushion ball
Foot on top of ball   of foot   between arms   on chest

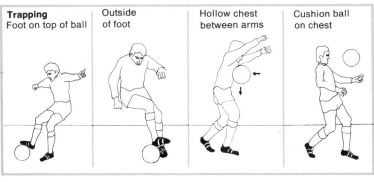

Kicking   Side foot pass   Chip kick   Outside
Instep kick   for rising ball   foot: before

Outside   Side foot volley   **Shooting** Volley   Side volley
foot: after

Throwing in

Tackling Front block tackle

Shoulder charge

Slide block tackle

Goalkeeping
One-handed throw

Body behind the ball

Picking up ball

Tipping wet ball over bar

Catching ball in air

Catching passing shot in arc

and accuracy. It is very like punching the ball but using the neck instead of the fist. Timing is obviously a highly essential factor; just when to leap, keeping both eyes rigidly on the ball, is probably more important than the actual contact itself. After a bit of practice, it will be possible to direct the ball in various directions simply flicking the head to the right or left. In a general mêlée of players, it is vital to jump as high as you can. Strikers should remember to head down in front of goal, or otherwise the ball often will go over the bar. Defenders should obviously head the ball up to clear the opposing forwards.

A good and obvious way to practise heading is to go out with a friend and try heading the ball backwards and forwards to each other. Tennis with foreheads, not rackets, is another excellent form of training, across a centre net. A good header of the ball must be an accurate header of the ball.

Dribbling Master dribblers of the ball like Stanley Matthews and George Best perfected the art of beating two or three men, while at the same time knowing exactly when to release the ball with maximum effect to a colleague. Greedy dribblers dribble on and on and finally get beaten: they can be harmful and destructive to their team. Dribbling requires perfect balance and an ability to carry the ball with both the inside and the outside of the foot. An elusive style of body swerve is also essential: a full-back will often be beaten by the feint of the hips or a ball pushed by his wrong foot. A brilliant winger like Garrincha of Brazil had such tremendous acceleration that he could beat two or three defenders in one burst over thirty yards. Always try and catch your opponent on the wrong foot—and when bringing the ball up to him, always delay running past until he is about to tackle. That will mean he has less time to recover and put him out of the game for a few extra and very precious seconds. Dribbling is one of the great showpieces of soccer—but over-indulgence can be fatal.

Trapping A ball falling from the skies must be brought under control by a player with his foot or chest or it will simply bounce away to an opponent. Trapping requires a certain amount of skill but it is not as difficult as it seems. The main thing to remember is that the sole of the foot should be placed firmly on top of the ball as it hits the ground and it will inevitably stay 'dead'. This requires practice but it should not be too hard to master. Perfect balance is essential, and to aid it both arms should be outstretched.

An approaching ball which is too high to trap with the foot and too low to head should be cushioned by the chest. Here the chest should be hollowed between two arms so the ball drops down in front of the player. Another way is to lean right back to cushion the dropping ball, again with the chest. Both ways can be equally effective. Remember that after trapping the ball it is no good standing there and admiring the operation. A grateful opponent will be quick to take possession of the frozen ball. So speed off the mark is vital.

Kicking A professional footballer should be able to kick a ball equally well with either foot—although many have often neglected this art, even at the top level. You sometimes see talented foot-ballers transferring a ball to their stronger foot for a shot or a pass and therefore, in a few seconds, losing the element of surprise. Some of the worlds most dangerous centre forwards like Nat Lofthouse, the former Bolton and England player, have been able to shoot ferociously with either foot and their careers have advanced accordingly. But even though a minor player may carry on throughout his soccer career relying strictly on only one strong foot, he will at least profit by kicking the ball with accuracy and with the right timing.

The basic way to kick a ball is with the instep or inside of the foot. The instep (where the lace is) is the fundamental method and the toe punters will soon be found out because the ball will inevitably spoon away in any direction. In kicking the ball with the instep, the toe must be kept down so the instep comes up flat against the ball on impact. Kicking with the inside of the foot is more a gliding motion more suitable for a short ground pass or a scoring shot at goal from close range.

To keep the ball low for a shot at goal or a long pass along the ground, the head should be kept down and the knee of the striking leg kept over the ball on impact. The non-kicking leg should be beside the ball on connecting and the ball should be driven firmly forward. To make a ball rise in the air, the body should be lent back slightly on impact. There should be a firm follow through with the kicking leg and the ball will rise accordingly.

Passing Some teams, for instance Wolves in the 1950s, concentrated on long passing during their successful careers while others use multiple short passing movements to attack the opposing goal. The specialists have been able to build up their own

Top: Riva passing in the 1970 World
Cup semi-final of West Germany versus
Italy. Bottom: Bobby Charlton evades a
tackle and centres

advanced winning formulas through constant practice. A minor amateur team, on the other hand, will build a winning combination if it concentrates on doing things simply but well. Yet it is surprising how often the ball is passed to the enemy by inaccurate, thoughtless kicking or through sloppy lobs across the field.

Passing with the inside or outside of the foot The inside of the foot method is the popular method for pushing the ball to a colleague over short distances. The ball should be hit firmly with the centre of the foot, which should be an inch or two off the ground This is a good way to retain accuracy. To keep the ball on the ground, there should be a firm follow-through with the kicking foot and both legs should be bent. The head should be kept down. The outside of the foot method is not so popular but it is a useful device of knocking the ball away to a colleague on the outside before being tackled or for dribbling round an opponent. The outside method requires a great deal of practice but is useful in tight situations.

The long pass The most popular method of passing the ball long distance is in the air and this is effected by the **chip-pass** method. The ball should be lofted above the opposition's heads, but not too high because it will then carry beyond reach of a team-mate. A long ball along the ground can be used dangerously but it requires tremendous accuracy and there is always the chance the opposition will be in the ball's path. An accurate chip can be carried out with the inside of the big toe and a good follow-through will guarantee distance. Ideal long passes are made from either wing catching an opposing full-back out of position. **Chip-passing** is really made up of an elegant stab with the foot which directs the ball in a curving flight just enough to clear the opposition's heads. The chip can also be done over short distances but the ball has to be hit delicately and precisely to escape an opponent.

Other methods of passing are through side-foot volleying and back-heeling. **Back-heeling** requires a certain instinctive sense and should be used only by a player when he senses a gap behind him and a colleague handily placed.

Side-foot volleying is an ideal method of trapping the ball and passing it in one movement. A ball approaching below waist level should be cushioned with the inside of the foot, the leg bent to the required height. The ball should then be pushed on to a team mate.

Penalty kicks These are usually taken by the most accurate shot in the team. They should also be taken by a player able to keep calm in a fraught situation. A penalty kick might be awarded with a minute to go with no goals previously scored—so the kicker will have to be equipped with good nerves. The best penalty kicks are directed *low* into goal just inside one of the uprights which will not give the goalkeeper much chance of making contact. The ball should be driven hard, especially on muddy grounds.

Throw-ins These should be taken with both hands, the ball passing from behind and over the head—otherwise a foul throw will be given by the referee. Both feet should also be on the ground when the throw is made. The strength of the throw will depend on the force of the throwing arms and a strong driving swing from the waist. A throw-in expert can gain distance by taking a small run beforehand but his feet must remain on the ground. His team mates must try to move into open space for one of them to take his throw, though opponents will inevitably crowd them. A crafty throw-in will put the ball where the opposition least expect. Taking throw-ins is an art of deception.

Corner kicks These are usually taken by wingers or strong place-kickers. They should always be approached at an angle to the ball placed by the corner flag: if the kick is made after a straight approach the ball will not swerve. The toe of the boot should meet the underside of the ball to give a good lift towards the opponent's goal; perfect body balance while taking the kick is essential. Corner kicks are usually 'outswingers' taken with the right boot from the righthand corner flag, or vice versa; or they are 'in-swingers' taken with the right boot from the left hand corner flag, or vice versa. Inswingers can be very effective in swerving the ball close to goal while outswingers can instigate a dangerous header from the edge of the box. Corner kicks should be varied— a lowish cross to the near post can give a defence a load of trouble. That is why a defence must always have their full-backs covering the far and near post to stop possible headers or deflections which have beaten the goalkeeper.

Shooting Profuse goalscorers are usually equipped with some uncanny instinct in their make-up which makes the job look easy. Jimmy Greaves, for one, could push a shot past a goalkeeper with such ease that he might have been posting a letter. But the fact that he may have beaten two or three men in the process, plus one of the best goalkeepers in the country, was a reminder that few others could have begun the process at all. Greaves certainly had a natural instinct for scoring and was the first to admit it. But for the raw striker, there are ways of improving the art of goal-scoring, practice, of course, being vitally important.

A striker will improve the accuracy of his shooting by spending a few hours each week hitting a ball at a friend in goal. A couple of coats in a local park will do the trick—but the more advanced player may have access to a shooting box installed at top pro-fessional or amateur clubs. This will give him the opportunity of taking rebounds off a wooden or concrete wall. The ball will come at him from all directions and the striker will have ample oppor-tunity of practising the instep drive, the volley and the half volley.

The **instep drive**, to send the ball low and wide of a goalkeeper, is carried out in the same way as described in the Kicking section. The main thing is to keep one's eyes on the ball—there should be a good follow-through after making contact with the instep.

Gordon Banks of Stoke City and
England leaps towards a header by
Dyson of Tottenham Hotspur

Remember a goalkeeper will also be beaten through strength of
the shot, so maximum force, particularly from outside the penalty
box, is essential. A ground drive, taken on the run, can be very
effective if given an extra element of surprise. A goalkeeper, un-
sighted by his defence, might suddenly be confronted by a passing
low shot before he can make a dive.

High shots with the instep, lobs and chips can all be effective
but goalkeepers are more prone to save shots coming in under
the crossbar. For accuracy, it is best to veer the shot towards the
angles of the crossbar and the upright.

The **volley** shot is taken when the ball is still in the air. It is a
very useful method for taking rebounds off the crossbar or for
lowish centres.

In the case of the ball coming straight at the striker he should
contact the ball when it is about a foot off the ground and, keeping
the knee well over the ball, drive in a shot. Low centres coming in
from the right or left should be met with a **side-volley**—the body
leaning away from the ball and the shooting foot swinging on to
and connecting with the ball at the full stretch. The **half volley** is
taken when the ball has already hit the ground. Contact should be
made almost immediately.

Heading at goal is an essential method of scoring and usually
comes from centres or lobs across goal and corner kicks. A good
header of the ball will be able to outjump the rival defence and be
able to direct his shot off the forehead down into the opposing
goal. He should always head the ball down or else the ball may
go over the crossbar. Maximum force is obtained with the neck
muscles, the ball directed towards the stanchion of the net. To
gain height, a striker should make his run and jump from the far
edge of the box and start climbing towards the oncoming ball.

These are the most general methods of scoring, but goals can
also be scored accidentally by deflections off shins, ankles, knees,
noses and other parts of the body. It is always important for a
striker to follow up a shot in case a goalkeeper fumbles the ball.

Many goals are scored by players running in on the near or far post to deflect a team mate's pass. Good strikers are those who always create space for themselves in the opposing goal area and build up attacks by laying the ball off to the wings or a better placed colleague down the centre. Reliable strikers should be strong enough to run a ball through a defence without being knocked off the ball and when the goalkeeper comes out, either to kick it or to side-foot it past him. They should take up position on the blindside of the defence remembering to keep *onside*, particularly from free kicks. *They should never hesitate to shoot.* A couple of shots over the bar early on might bring better things later on. Goalscoring is a matter of confidence—with confidence goalscoring comes easily. Without it, weeks can go by without a striker hitting the net.

Tackling The main legitimate ways of robbing the opponent of the ball are by the front block tackle, the slide tackle and the slide block tackle—it is against the laws to tackle a player from *behind* or leap at him with two feet. Tackling requires confidence and a bold approach but a good tackler will rarely injure himself badly on making contact. It is a matter of split-second timing, keeping an eye firmly on the ball, tensing the muscles and not changing one's mind. A bad tackler will go in with his eyes half closed hoping for the best—and find his opponent has dummied past him.

Novice tacklers often fail because they either go in too early or too late. The most popular form of tackling is the **front block**. When an opponent approaches, a defender should go forward and try to win possession by firmly blocking the ball with his right or left foot. Contact will probably mean that the man in possession falls slightly off balance and the ball becomes the property of the tackler.

The **slide tackle** is chiefly used by defenders on opponents building up attacks along the wings. It is ideal on wet surfaces because the tackle is usually made from a seated position on the ground. In going in for the ball slightly ahead of the man in possession, the tackler should accelerate forward and drop on his right or left side and sweep the ball away with toe or instep. The **sliding block tackle** is similar, except the opponent will actually be tackled in possession of the ball from a seated position. Another form of robbing an opponent in desperate situations is to drop on one knee as an opponent is about to run past and push the ball to a colleague.

Shoulder charging is an acceptable form of robbing an opponent of the ball—although it is less popular in Latin countries. A good old English shoulder charge could knock an opponent off the ball but arms and elbows should not be used. Over-zealousness here could cost the exponent a free kick.

Running off the ball One often sees schoolboy games in which all the players merge on the ball together, all trying to get a boot at it. This, of course, is wrong—soccer is a simple game and to play it well, players should sense where to take up positive positions off the ball when a colleague is in possession. It is no good crowding round him waiting for a pass; the intelligent player off the ball will make space for himself and look for the most potentially destructive unmanned area in which to receive a pass. It is possible for players off the ball to draw the opposition away from the defending goal by running wide, so affording to the man in possession a gap to take the ball through. But it is no use dashing off blindly in any direction in the hope of having the ball sent through. A player should keep his eye on a colleague with the ball throughout. He should try and help him, not hinder him by running offside or into a defensive trap.

Training Many amateur players often find it hard to devote much time to extensive training but even a couple of hours each week will be of great help. Long distance running helps to build up stamina while an hour or two of shooting practice could make all the difference. It is useful to go out into a park with a friend and practise heading a ball to each other. If there is an opportunity for head tennis, so much the better. Dribbling and short sprints are essential and attackers and defenders should practise speed on the turn, which is vital. Short backward sprints facing are also handy for defenders over distances of 15 yards. Forwards should practise dribbling round posts. Practice games are also important and park games go on all around the year with an abundance of volunteers ready to join in. An inexperienced player without a club will often find himself signed up to play proper games for a club if he displays some talent in the park. Some modest club teams are often short of players and on the look out for new ones. So the park is the factory floor of certain sections of Sunday amateur football.

Goalkeeping The most individual and specialized player in the team is a goalkeeper. His job enjoys a unique element in that he can use his hands to stop the ball and pick it up. He is his own master of his side's goal net and penalty area; he wears a jersey, cap and, on wet days, gloves. His chosen position has even been described as 'crazy'! Goalkeepers are generally born and not made, for the job not only requires a great deal of natural elasticity but a total dictatorship and knowledge of his own goal area. Leading international goalkeepers like Lev Yashin of Russia, Ricardo Zamora of Spain and Frank Swift of England all mixed a kind of eccentricity and showmanship with their trade in their time—while more recently Gordon Banks, England's goalkeeper in two World Cups, helped modernize the art.

Goalkeeping is not simply standing between the goal posts waiting for a shot and returning the ball aimlessly downfield. Banks, and Swift before him, showed the value of setting up attacks by throwing the ball quickly to an unmarked defender.

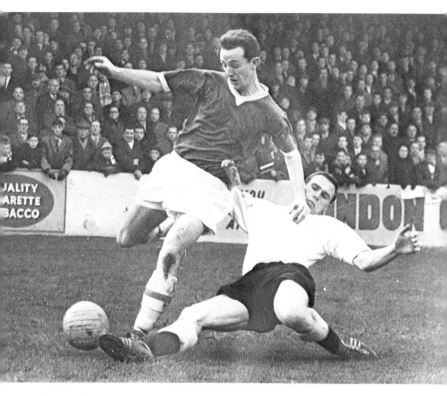

By earlier standards a perfect slide
tackle by Ray Wilson of Huddersfield,
who played for England in 1966. But
what would the referee give today?

These throws are highly effective and can catch an attacking
team off guard. The ball should be thrown one-handed, firmly and
low to a team mate's feet; constant practice will increase the
distance a goalkeeper can reach. Under the new rule, a forward
can no longer charge a goalkeeper but he can stand in front of
him and make clearing difficult. In this case, it is best for a goalkeeper to nip the ball quickly away from the forward into an open
space and then punt it away downfield towards a colleague. But
remember, a goalkeeper can only take *four* steps with the ball
between rolling it along the ground. A good goalkeeper will have
a strong long-distance kicking ability and be able to make the
halfway line with his punts and goalkicks.

A goalkeeper's chief role lies in his ability to stop the ball. A
shot can fly in from all angles—high and low—and a goalkeeper
should adopt various positions to take them. *Safety first* should be
a goalkeeper's first motto—body behind the ball, eyes firmly on
it.

Direct ground shots along the ground may seem rather easier
to deal with but a goalkeeper who stands there with his legs open,

Left: Come out and get it! Gordon Banks shows Martin Chivers of Tottenham Hotspur who's in charge of the penalty area. Right: Lev Yashin makes a spectacular save against a West German free kick at Goodison Park, Liverpool in July 1966. All the elasticity of a world-class goalkeeper is displayed

eyes off the ball, watching the opposition, may make a terrible blunder and let the ball roll under him into the net. In taking these low shots, it is best to drop on one knee and, with both hands, scoop up the ball firmly to the chest. Another popular way is to bend down as if touching the toes, knees slightly bent and both feet together, with both palms open towards the ball. On contact, the ball should roll up the arms and be clutched quickly to the chest. With shots coming directly in at chest height, a goalkeeper should jump so that he gathers the ball at stomach level and then transfer the ball to his chest. The jump will afford extra protection and prevent a rebound.

High balls directly under the bar should be viewed with great caution. The day before writing this section, I was guilty of a gross error of judgement by letting in a long high shot from 30 yards which I should certainly have turned over the bar. My first mistake was being caught too far off my goal line, the second was timing my jump too soon. The ball sailed over my head into the net. Calamity! Goalkeepers should always make up their mind quickly on how to deal with such shots. On a wet day, one should flick the ball one-handed over the bar, though normally it is sounder to catch the ball and so prevent a corner. The catching hands should always grasp the ball towards the back of the ball, which prevents it slipping through.

A goalkeeper should have the confidence to come out and catch high centres and corners. An unconfident goalkeeper will punch everything away, often to a member of the opposition. So it is vitally important to come out and grab these balls before an opponent can head towards goal. And a defence will help its goalkeeper by allowing him space to do so. A goalkeeper who can't reach a ball from a corner may let in a goal because his mates have crowded him out.

A nasty shot to save is that directed to the farthest corner of the goal away from the goalkeeper. This will inevitably require an extravagant dive of the spectacular type the crowds love. To do this the goalkeepers must thrust hard into orbit with the legs, reaching the ball with one or two hands or fists. The two-armed dive is a quick and sound method of pushing the ball away from goal, two hands always being better than one. In catching a fast-moving knee-high shot, the modern way is to pounce like a springing panther in a downward arc across goal towards the ball and, after clutching it, allowing the under forearm and the ball to make the first ground contact. The ball should be grabbed to the chest immediately after hitting the ground. This is a rather more advanced speciality.

Positioning is all important. When an opposing forward runs through on his own, a goalkeeper will inevitably let in a goal if he stands there waiting on his goal line. He instead must advance towards the player to narrow the angle: it is extraordinary how small a goal will seem to a forward if he sees a goalkeeper running towards him off his line—it will literally shrink and give him very little room to shoot into. This is so particularly at angles sideways to the goal. A goalkeeper should know just when to come out for the ball, and when it is a loose ball he should inform his defenders that the ball is 'mine'. When a forward breaks through and all seems lost, a goalkeeper should plunge sideways at his feet protecting himself with his shoulders while grabbing the ball. A goalkeeper should be the thorough commander of his area and let his colleagues know exactly what he is going to do. It is often wise to make a mark on the 6-yard line dead opposite the centre of the goal to act as a landmark in taking up the appropriate position. It will help guide a goalkeeper who has moved too far to the right or left of goal to receive a shot.

Remember that excessive showmanship is not a wise thing for a goalkeeper but, on the other hand, a goalkeeper should never be dull. He should combine his duties as safely as possible, at the same time diving about like an elastic clown in desperate situations.

6 TACTICS

Since the evolution of soccer back in the 1860s, when new laws began to be drawn up and teams decided that eleven perspiring men on each side were the ideal number to make up a game, managers and clubs, coaches and countries have been continuously occupied in thinking up new ways of making goals while keeping the opposition out of their own end. New rules, like the changing of the offside law in 1866–67 and again in 1925, require new tactics.

One of the most influential and successful methods was the third back game or W formation created by Herbert Chapman, the Arsenal manager, to counter the new offside law in the 1920s. The 4—2—4 formation, used so flamboyantly by the Brazilians in 1958, also had great impact. In the case of the W formation used by English teams before and after the Second World War, it was the adventurous Hungarians who made the system redundant, while 4—2—4 tended to be superseded in the 1960s and 1970s by 4—3—3 and the even more defensive 4—4—2.

Some of the first major tactics were born in the early matches between England and Scotland in the 1870s. In 1872 England used a goalkeeper, a full back, a half back and eight forwards. The Scotland team had two half backs and seven forwards. The result was 0—0. The English relied heavily on the dribbling game, in which one player would set off like a hare and try and force the ball through the opposing defence. Eventually the Scots decided that team work would have better effect, and invented a system of passing which proved devastating. England were trounced at first by such skilful teamwork: one journalist summed up Scotland's 3—1 victory at Kennington Oval by noting that the visitors' 'passing was extremely good, and it would have been better if some of their opponents [England] had pursued the same tactics, instead of selfishly keeping the ball until it was too late . . .'

In time England learnt their lesson, and with 2—3—5 (including an attacking centre half) becoming an accepted team formation towards the end of the century, they often countered the scientific methods employed by the Scots. But the Scottish style was to influence European countries like Austria and Hungary, where an English coach, Jimmy Hogan, had gone to preach the classical Scottish way.

Famous English teams like Newcastle, Aston Villa and Preston North End all exploited close-pattern-weaving football but it came to an end in 1925 when the offside rule was changed. Defenders had been constantly catching rival attacks offside and goals had become scarcer and scarcer, so the law was altered to make it only necessary for two players, as against three previously, to be between the attacker and the opposing goal line when the ball was last played. This allowed an epidemic of scoring and teams had to quickly adopt new tactics to counter the new rule. The attacking centre half gave way to the defensive or stopper centre half. This became known as the third back game. A typical Arsenal formation in the thirties would include two full backs marking the opposing wingers, a stopper centre half marking the centre forward, two wing halves marking the inside forwards, two raiding wingers, two scheming inside forwards feeding their wingers and a brave centre forward to knock the goals in.

Italy, Austria and some South American countries persisted with the attacking centre half game, Italy with notable success, twice winning the World Cup in 1934 and 1938. After the Second World War, the old W formula served England until Hungary, employing a deep-lying centre forward in Hidegkuti, cut it to ribbons at Wembley in 1953.

In 1958, Brazil won the World Cup in Sweden using a fluent 4—2—4 system with four men at the rear, inside forward Didi and one of the wing halves, Zito, in mid-field as linkmen. With the brilliant winger Garrincha making goals for the central strikers, Pele and Vava, the system worked almost perfectly in the final, when Sweden were beaten 5—2. Four years later in the World Cup in Chile, Brazil altered their tactics when Pele was injured and unable to play in the final rounds. Outside left Zagalo dropped back to mid-field creating a 4—3—3 line up but Brazil, though slightly more cautious, easily won the final against the Czechs.

By the time of the 1966 Finals in England, Garrincha had lost his speed, Pele was again chopped down, this time by the Portuguese, and it was the hard, muscular sides who finally reached the final. Sir Alf Ramsay, lacking a fast winger in the league of Garrincha, chose 4—3—3 as his system for the finals and it won the day against West Germany. This formation became known as Alf's 'wingless wonders' and although it pulled off the World Cup the tactics became an all too dreary feature of English football in the late sixties. The formation was taken up eagerly by timid managers frightened of defeat and bored spectators to tears, since without wingers the success of the style was dependent on crab-like build-ups.

Worse was to come with the arrival of 4—4—2 (with only two forward strikers), a system employed by England in Mexico. It was therefore refreshing to see Brazil reverting to 4—2—4 in these finals and winning them in exuberant style against Italy, the past masters of *catenaccio*, or 'eiderdown' defence, the most negative system of all in that it included a defensive sweeper and four backs in front.

Since then, there have been signs of a return to attacking football—and wingers. Ajax of Amsterdam and West Germany have introduced a system of 'total' football in which the ten men on the outfield are encouraged to take part in an all-round offensive. The system could be translated as a very flexible 4—3—3 played by masters like Beckenbauer, an attacking sweeper, Cruyff, Muller, Breitner and Krol. Aggression has retrieved the spectator sport.

Basic positions in a 4–2–4 system (top)
and a 4–3–3 system (bottom)

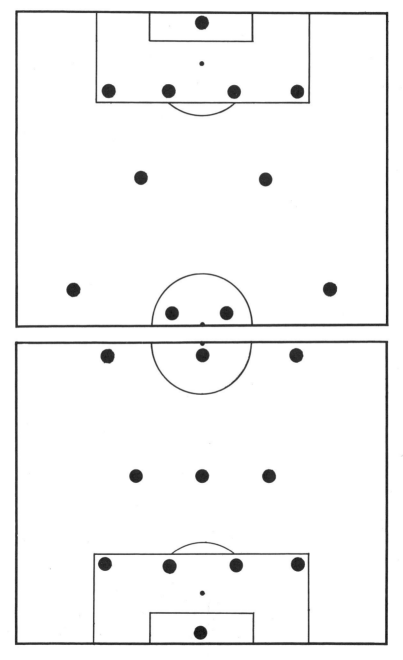

7 SOME FAMOUS MATCHES

England 1 Scotland 5—31 March 1928, Wembley Stadium, London
Of all the many contests between England and Scotland, this particular one has gone down in history as being the most conclusive for the victors and the most embarrassing for the losers. It was a total annihilation and earned the Scottish team the everlasting, much merited accolade—the title of the 'Wembley Wizards'.

A galaxy of attractive celtic skills overpowered a mercenary England side on that rainy afternoon once the opening hands had been shown and the first furrows etched brown on a spongy green surface. Scotland pitched in with some of the most elusive ball players in soccer history: Alex James, Alan Morton, Jimmy Gibson, Hugh Gallacher and Alec Jackson; they fizzed, wove tender patterns, formed spaces which initially seemed to be guarded by lumbering England defenders but were uncorked by passes measured to the exact fatal inch.

One English critic wrote after the match: 'We were like the man who saw a giraffe for the first time and said defensively that there was no such animal.' There had certainly been no reason to expect such a thrashing beforehand in the English camp. A year before England had won up at Hampden Park by 2—1, so a fairly close game was expected with the odds in favour of the home team.

But Alec Jackson, the 'laughing cavalier' of Huddersfield Town (he was transferred later to Chelsea), proved to be one of the main artificers of England's defeat. Imagine him now, with that daunting smile slipping across his cheeks, dashing to turn in a cross from Morton in the first half, for Scotland's opening goal. In the second half, Jackson scored one goal with a header and another with a volley of astounding force. James and Gibson scored other goals for Scotland as the England team began to trail after the ball like old men searching for lost farthings on their hands and knees. Kelly did manage to score England's only goal near the end, but England and their famous centre forward Dixie Dean were firmly and totally eclipsed.
Teams: England—Hufton, Goodall, Jones, Edwards, Wilson, Healless, Hulme, Kelly, Dean, Bradford, Smith.
Scotland—J. D. Harkness, Nelson, Law, Gibson, Bradshaw, McMullen, Jackson, Dunn, Gallacher, James, A. Morton.

Italy 0 England 4—16 May 1948, Municipal Stadium, Turin
Few matches in Italy aroused more frenzied interest beforehand than this confrontation between the 1938 World Cup holders and the side whose ancestors had pioneered modern soccer. Ten years, incorporating a world war and defeat for Benito Mussolini, had passed since Italy won the World Cup in Paris. The Municipal Stadium in Turin, where 75,000 fanatics gathered on a sizzling hot afternoon to view the execution of sedate old England, had been originally named Mussolini Stadium.

The Italians fielded an excellent team built round a nucleus of Juventus players (who only a few months later would be killed in an air crash, a disaster which would prove calamitous for Italy in the 1950 World Cup). When the England team took the field in the enervating heat, Billy Wright noted what first-class athletes the Italians looked in their 'blue, tight-fitting singlets and abbreviated white shorts'. When the teams lined up for the national anthem, there were a number of familiar faces in the England side including the captain and goalkeeper Frank Swift, Stanley Matthews and Tom Finney.

The Italians toed the pitch in anticipation like mountain ponies but it was England who broke out and scored a goal which is still discussed and hailed to this day in Turin. It came after four minutes and was contrived from a fairly innocent situation after Wright had brought the ball out of defence and passed the ball forward to Matthews. Normally the 'prince of dribblers' would have been expected to shuffle forward on one of his long runs; the Italian defence paused but Stanley, spying a gap behind the Italian left back, Eliani, sent a precise pass through to Stan Mortensen galloping downfield in a blur of black and white.

The tall, immensely powerful Italian half, Parola, tore out towards the touchline but just before he tackled the Blackpool player, Mortensen unleashed a shot from almost the dead-ball line and the ball sped like a silver bullet straight into the top near corner of Bacigalupo's goal. It was one of the most stunning of all goals but one which Mortensen would modestly describe as a bit of a fluke. He had seen the Italian goalkeeper coming off the line to take a probable centre to Lawton and he managed to put the ball into a gap behind him. Before half time Mortensen made exactly the same run but instead of shooting, he pulled the ball back to Lawton to shoot the ball in from close range.

The Italian crowd were naturally petrified by the way the game had veered away from their national favourites. They screamed and whistled for a revival and for a long period the balance of power was perilously close to changing hands. But Swift made some unbelievable saves, including one amazing snatch at the feet of the elusive Italian left winger, Carapellese. When Swift was not in a position to stop the shots the full backs Scott and Howe did so with goal line clearances. The Italians had to acknowledge fate was against them when Gabetto headed a free

kick from Mazzola's free kick on to the underside of the crossbar. Swift managed to leap across the goal and catch the ball before any Italian could stab it in. The Italian players were almost in tears. Two Italian goals disallowed by the Spanish referee frustrated the whistling crowd even more.

Intermittently doused down from the touchline with soda syphons in the second half by their manager Vittorio Pozzo, the Italians fought bravely on but near the end, Finney popped in two exquisite goals. After the match Swift shook his team mates by the hand in the dressing room—'You've made me the proudest man alive.' England had indeed won a famous victory against a side endowed with both skill and creative flair.

Italy—Bacigalupo, Ballarin, Eliani, Anrovazzi, Parola, Grezar, Menti, Loik, Gabetto, Mazzola, Carapellese.

England—Swift, Scott, Howe, Wright, Franklin, Cockburn, Matthews, Mortensen, Lawton, Mannion, Finney.

United States 1 England 0—29 June 1950, Belo Horizonte, Brazil (World Cup)

This match has been quoted as 'the most humiliating defeat English football has ever suffered'. It got relatively little publicity in the United States—but when the result was broadcast in England, many people believed the announcer was either drunk or suffering from sunstroke. Sober, he reiterated the result: 'England 0, the United States 1, repeat 1.'

A team of well-meaning triers, who admitted before the game they had no chance of drawing, let alone winning, had pulled off one of the most astonishing results in football. England had flown into the dusty mining town of Belo Horizonte as one of the favourites to win the 1950 World Cup in Brazil. Little was known about the United States except they were captained by Eddie McIlvenny, a Scot, who had been given a free transfer from the Third Division club, Wrexham. And yet . . .

The dressing room facilities were regarded by the English party and manager Walter Winterbottom as sub-standard after Rio de Janeiro's so the team changed before the game at the Minas Athletic Club. The Americans changed at the ground. They were not too fussy. What did it matter when they were going to get a thorough hiding?

When the England team arrived they looked as formidable as a

Roman legion. Many English supporters connected with the mining community were sitting in the stands looking forward to a barrage of goals from Mortensen, Finney, Mullen and the rest against a side who had been invited to take part in the World Cup finals simply to make up numbers. The English press sharpened their pencils and drew little boxes in their note books to record a dozen or so England goals. Somehow, England failed to score in the first minute; but how many amateur tipsters that day backed them not to score in ninety minutes? As it was, England had as many chances as there are peas in a tin; the United States had one and scored. It came five minutes before half-time when centre forward Gaetjens headed past the mortified Williams from a right-wing centre. After that, England became more and more desperate but try as they might, they could not score. Two shots hit the post, one shot by Mullen looked well over the line and Mortensen was brought down by a rugby tackle on his way to goal. When the whistle went, McIlvenny, a true hero, was chaired off the field by a jubilant crowd.

Wright put down his team's defeat to 'over-anxiousness'. Certainly if the England forwards had been steadier with their shooting and not resorted to panicky over-elaboration the day would have been theirs. A subsequent defeat by Spain put England out of the World Cup. They had come as one of the favourites and went home as something of a joke. As for the United States team, their win did little to inspire a new soccer craze in their country. Only now, as soccer begins to boom there, are a new generation of American fans beginning to compare the Horizonte result as an event comparable to the Boston Tea Party.

United States—Borghi, Keough, Maca, McIlvenny, Colombo, Bahr, Wallace, Pariani, Gaetjens, J. Souza, A. Souza.
England—Williams, Ramsey, Aston, Wright, Hughes, Dickinson, Finney, Mortensen, Bentley, Mannion, Mullen.

Blackpool 4 Bolton 3—1953 F.A. Cup Final, Wembley
The Coronation Cup Final will stand in posterity as 'the Matthews final'. On a glorious May afternoon, Matthews like an orange tarantula preyed upon the weary frame of Bolton during the last twenty minutes of play to convert imminent defeat into a Black-pool victory. The magic of those twenty minutes, which an injury-stricken Bolton side started leading 3—1, only to lose 4—3, is commemorated as one of the legends of the game.

Matthews had twice before been to Wembley to play in a Cup Final—in 1948 and 1951—but each time Blackpool had lost, first to Manchester United in an outstanding match, and then against Newcastle. But when Blackpool stepped out on the Wembley pitch for the third time, few people doubted they would not win a medal for Stanley. They had the talent, the players and Matthews to overcome a pedestrian opposition. But as so often happens in tense matches of this kind, Blackpool found themselves a goal down very early on; their quiveringly tense goalkeeper Farm allowed a dolly shot from Lofthouse to go through his hands.

The first half generally favoured the sturdy Bolton side. Matthews was rarely in possession and Moir scored a second goal for Bolton after Mortensen had equalized with a shot deflected in by Hassall. When Bell, limping like a steeplechaser with a fractured limb, managed to head another goal for Bolton in the second half, there seemed little chance that Matthews could net his elusive butterfly.

The minutes ticked on, nervous groups of men nibbled scones and cushions in front of their television sets; with half an hour to go Banks, as well as Bell, was limping. But for some reason Bolton kept Banks at left back and it would cost them the Final. Taylor, a splendid performer, and Fenton began coaxing the ball through to Matthews and at last he opened his surprise gift box.

In a smooth flow came a Matthews mixture of wiggles, feints, darts, gallops, sudden halts, shuffles, shuffles to the right, shuffles to the left, hands held out with fingers dangling for perfect balance.

With twenty minutes to go, Matthews shot his first telling bolt. A lofted centre to the far post had Hanson groping at the ball—but a princess's glove patting a gamekeeper's shoulder was about the impact the goalkeeper's fist had on the ball. It fell at Mortensen's feet and a stab of a boot made the score 3—2, still in Bolton's favour. Despite waves of Blackpool pressure, Bolton held on to their lead until three minutes from the end. Mortensen was fouled on the edge of the box and took the kick himself from twenty yards range. Hanson stared up at the frenzied stands as Mortensen's shot eluded his white defensive wall and sailed into the net.

That was surely it. Extra time was now a near certainty until Matthews decided patience was decidedly not a virtue. Away he

went again, up the right from Taylor's pass, drew Barrass to him and centred straight across the Bolton goal. In the sudden, total silence, Perry aimed his shot firm and true and the kneeling, trembling, well-beaten goalkeeper Hanson confirmed there was a ball in the Bolton net. The rejoicing which followed evokes memories of a fiesta: a thunderous salute to one of the great sporting heroes. Even the Bolton team applauded when Harry Johnston accepted the Cup from the Queen. It was very easy to forget the Bolton players but they had been part of Stanley Matthew's stage, and how bravely they trod it.

Blackpool—Farm, Shimwell, Garrett, Fenton, Johnston, Robinson, Matthews, Taylor, Mortensen, Mudie, Perry.

Bolton—Hanson, Ball, Banks, Wheeler, Barrass, Bell, Holden, Moir, Lofthouse, Hassall, Langton.

England 3 Hungary 6—25 November 1953, Wembley

The match in which the buoyant Hungarian 'Magyars' did English football a favour. A certain smugness still hung over the old masters of soccer before the arrival of Puskas and his team at Wembley Stadium. The majority of the English press failed to grasp the danger; they decreed England would not lose their unbeaten home record against foreign teams at Wembley. Only one football correspondent disagreed, predicting a score line of Hungary 4, England 2.

He got near enough to the final shattering result although one doubts whether he envisaged just how devastating would be the Hungarian superiority. The Hungarians only took sixty seconds to score. The England defence was quickly cut apart and Hidegkuti blazed a shot into the roof of Merrick's net.

That goal had a paralyzing effect on England. They were simply not prepared for the Hungarian tactics, now popularly known as 4-2-4, with Hidegkuti (a deep-lying centre forward) and the stolidly consistent Bozsik causing most of the damage from mid-

field. Harry Johnston, the England centre half, peered around in vain for the man whom he was supposed to mark but Hidegkuti was usually operating wild and untrammelled round the pitch. Up front, Kocsis and Puskas, as the two main strikers, made the England goalkeeper's hands quiver each time he touched their thunderbolts from foot and head; on the wings, Czibor and Budai were effective in decoying the England full backs Ramsey and Eckersley away from the central firing zone. The England side that day must have felt they were in an abstract cloud cuckoo land in which they were required to mark a company of invisible men; but the prowess of the 1952 Olympic champions had been on record for some time—England's great fault lay in assuming that they were equal to the threat.

They did manage to equalize early on when Mortensen sent Sewell darting through. But from then on England were overwhelmed, while the Hungarians had built up a 4—2 lead by half time as Hidegkuti and Puskas twice capped a single goal by Mortensen. In the second half Bozsik and the Hidegkuti again hit another pair, and as poor old England stumbled nearing the end, dizzy and despairing, Ramsey popped one in from the penalty spot. There was beauty in all the Hungarian goals, but perhaps the most vivid in the memory was a left-footed shot on the turn by Puskas which had Merrick groping after the ball's disappearing blur like an old swan with a broken wing.

There was a chance for England to take revenge on the defeat
in the return at Budapest the following May, but the Hungarians
won even more emphatically by 7—1. Poor goalkeeper Merrick—
having received six goals at Wembley, they put him back in goal
again in the return match. He must have had nightmares about
Hidegkuti, Puskas and company for years afterwards.
England—Merrick, Ramsey, Eckersley, Wright, Johnston, Dickinson, Matthews, Taylor, Mortensen, Sewell, Robb.
Hungary—Grosics, Buzansky, Lantos, Bozsik, Lorant, Zakarias,
Budai, Kocsis, Hidegkuti, Puskas, Czibor.

Arsenal 4 Manchester United 5—5 February 1958, Highbury
The majority of First Division matches in England generally
fluctuate between the good and the bad, unless a team in the class
of Tottenham, Liverpool, Leeds or Manchester United are having
one of their majestic runs. Then their supporters can expect
something rather higher in quality at their home grounds every
fortnight. The great matches, the ones you remember all your life,
are but a tiny minority out of a myriad of forgotten games.

One such was the meeting between Arsenal and Manchester
United—the 'Busby Babes'—on a grey afternoon in February,
1958. The Babes came down from the north with an already
tremendous reputation earned by over two years of splendid
achievement. Their opponents were only having a moderate,
middle-of-the-table season and there seemed little chance they
would offer a major challenge to Matt Busby's team. But somehow
Arsenal, in a stirring second half, rose above themselves and
made this one of the most memorable league games of soccer
history.

It was also that splendid United team's last appearance together
in England before the team was halved in an air crash on a snow-
carpeted runway at Munich while flying home from a European
Cup match in Belgrade. The 64,000 spectators, who had seen
eleven very much alive United players stride arrogantly out of the
tunnel at Highbury, felt an immediate and appalling loss when the
news of the crash came through; the Babes had always looked so
indestructable, so full of life. It seemed inconceivable that half of
them had been suddenly extinguished, including the gargantuan
Duncan Edwards who died later in hospital. Bobby Charlton was
one of the few to survive.

The power of Edwards and his venerable partner, Eddie Colman, in the centre of the field put United in an almost impregnable
position before half time at Highbury. United ran the wings as well,
where the elusive Scanlon and Morgans wiggled and meandered
through the Arsenal defence. United's first goal of the match was
the supreme effort of the afternoon and was scored, predictably,
by Edwards.

When he ran up to take a free kick about twenty-five yards out-

Real Madrid's Hungarian star Ferenc
Puskas shoots his team's fifth goal
against Eintracht Frankfurt at Hampden
Park in May 1960

side the Arsenal penalty box, the goalkeeper he faced was Jack
Kelsey, a Welsh international, and considered one of the soundest
goalkeepers in the world. But Edwards curved his enormous
frame over the ball and drove it ferociously at surface level into the
far corner of the net. Kelsey dived gallantly but hopelessly in the
general direction of the whirling ball but he was much too late to
stop it. Two more goals by Bobby Charlton and Tommy Taylor
were added to the many problems Arsenal had to discuss at half
time. They were being annihilated.

The crowd were soon made aware of a new enthusiasm from
the underdogs. The half had hardly begun when Herd and Bloomfield twice created a surging, rolling wave of cheering around the
stadium. Arsenal's goals had all been scored in three minutes—
no wonder their captain, Dave Bowen, looked like a man with a
new fortune.

Although three goals in three minutes may have been enough
to unsettle some teams, yet Manchester United stayed true to
form. They reacted to the situation as would a rhinoceros on
being stung by a wasp. They looked calmly up at the Highbury
clock, observed there was still plenty of time to go and promptly
went to work again. Viollet and Taylor rolled in two further goals,
and although Tapscott brought Arsenal back into the proceedings
again with another stirring goal, the winners had reclaimed their
old composure. When the whistle came, the crowd cheered and
clapped and the players embraced for the joy of having partici-
pated in that exhilarating match.

Arsenal—Kelsey, Charlton, Evans, Ward, Fotheringham, Bowen,
Groves, Tapscott, Herd, Bloomfield, Nutt.

Manchester United—Gregg, Foulkes, Byrne, Colman, Jones,
Edwards, Morgans, Charlton, Taylor, Viollet, Scanlon.

Real Madrid 7 Eintracht Frankfurt 3—18 May 1960, Hampden Park, Glasgow (European Cup Final)

Genius is not easy to define in soccer but Real Madrid surely had
it that spring evening at Hampden when they lifted the art of soccer
to an almost unassailable height. They made it all look so ridicu-

lously easy; at times they made the West German team look like clowns, yet they were not: by any standards Eintracht were a strong team with an extremely dangerous centre forward in Stein. But progressively, their challenge waned against a side whose fluency of control and extraordinary teamwork over-whelmed and exhausted them.

As expected, di Stefano, Puskas and Gento, Real's renowned forward trio, were the main exponents of victory. But in addition to their own gilded mischief-making was the teamwork of the whole side knitted together in one moving, ramifying composition controlled from the centre. The defensive work of Pachin, Vidal and Santamaria, the promptings of Del Sol, the wing-running of Canario: all contributed to a blazing canvas.

Eintracht certainly started well enough, and the right-wing dashes of Kress often brought him hurtling through the Real defence, a feat quite remarkable for a 35-year-old veteran. He duly scored in the eighteenth minute and Real were forced to make an appraisal of their own play.

However, they were soon back in the game when Canario centred across the goal and di Stefano shot in the equalizer. Di Stefano's second curved past the tall, spindly Eintracht goal-keeper, Loy, only three minutes later. Poor Loy's expression grew longer and longer as the ever-increasing flood of Real attacks now began to bear down on him.

Soon after half time, Puskas scored from a narrow angle and then followed up with a short, sharp penalty. Real grew more and more reliant on close passing; a team mate was invariably there in a wide open space on their behalf; all he wanted was the ball and he invariably got it. Puskas hit two more forceful shots and Eintracht sagged like a burst balloon, but there were times when they summoned up a bit of wind to score. Stein managed to do so twice between Real attacks. Two final sights to savour remained: di Stefano fluttering like a white moth from the centre circle all the way downfield to score with a ground shot; and the 127,000 crowd waving farewell to the Real heroes as they ran round the pitch with their trophy at the close. Even after Real had left for the dressing rooms the massive crowd stayed to cheer on and on.
Real Madrid—Dominguez, Marquitos, Pachin, Vidal, Santa-maria, Zarraga, Canario, Del Sol, di Stefano, Puskas, Gento.
Eintracht—Loy, Lutz, Hoefer, Weilbacher, Eigenbrodt, Stinka, Kress, Lindner, Stein, Pfaff, Meier.

Sweden 2 Brazil 5—World Cup Final, June 1958, Rasunda Stadium, Stockholm

This was the World Cup Final in which a young Brazilian called Pele revealed his genius on the international circuit for the first time in scoring two extraordinary goals. Pele was the king after the match, weeping with emotion in the arms of his respectful

colleagues. But, in retrospect, his talents in this marvellous match should be seen as only part of the contribution made by a superb all-round team.

Sweden, watched by their own King and a totally unplacid, chanting Nordic crowd, had gone out for an early goal at the start hoping to disrupt the Brazilian side whose temperament had often let them down in previous World Cups. They duly got a goal within five minutes when Liedholm put the ball in the Brazilian net after a neat passing movement between Bergmark, Boerjesson and Simonsson. The Swedish coach, an Englishman named George Raynor, has said before the match that this was the incentive his side needed to win and with the prize claimed, Brazil were pinned back in defence.

The man who pulled them forward once more was a little man on the right wing called Garrincha (or Little Bird, as he was nick-named). He began to flash forward, bewildering the Swedish left back Axbom in spurts of yellow and green. After one such run, Garrincha stepped up his acceleration and crossed the ball into the penalty box, where Vava was waiting to smash the ball in, making the score 1—1. More and more of Garrincha dazzled the Swedes and now more and more of Pele. One of Pele's shots curled against a Swedish post and ricocheted out. Then Pele fed the ball to the sauntering mid-field 'Cobra' Didi, another exquisite pass found Garrincha, and Vava was waiting to push the ball home.

The poor Swedes were mesmerized as the Brazilian 4-2-4 formation rhythmically stroked the white ball from player to player and then suddenly accelerated it towards the goal. It represented spectacular individualism within the ordered structure of a great team and the football produced was of a brand one only sees two or three times in a lifetime.

Ten minutes after half time came a goal after which Pele ceased to be one member of the Brazilian team and became its champion knight for the future. After receiving Zagalo's cross, Pele played a little game of his own with the ball with his instep before flicking

Left: Mario Zagalo scoring in Brazil's World Cup win at Stockholm. Third from left is the young Pele. Below: Germany's second goal against England in the World Cup Final of 1966

it over Gustavsson and hitting it into the net. The crowd could scarcely believe its eyes. When Simonsson scored a splendid second goal for Sweden it only capped a mild period of relaxation by Brazil. Zagalo had already scored a fourth for Brazil, and then, during another frenzied period of merrymaking, Pele headed in a centre by Zagalo. At the end, the Brazilians did two laps of honour while their supporters chanted 'samba, samba'.

Sweden—Svensson, Bergmark, Axbom, Boerjesson, Gustavsson, Parling, Hamrin, Gren, Simonsson, Liedholm, Skoglund.

Brazil—Gilmar, D. Santos, N. Santos, Zito, Bellini, Orlando, Garrincha, Didi, Vava, Pele, Zagalo.

England 4 West Germany 2—World Cup Final, July 1966, Wembley Stadium

After four abortive and highly disappointing attempts, England at last succeeded in winning the World Cup for the first time in front of their own countrymen at Wembley. England were most fortunate in playing all their matches on their own favourite ground but this is not to throw doubt on their worthiness as winners, after beating Portugal in the semi-final and finally the hard, strong athletes from West Germany.

England came into the final without Jimmy Greaves, a move which not only shattered the morale of manager Alf Ramsey's most prolific goalscorers but also the confidence of many critics who felt the little man would be gravely missed in front of the German net.

But Ramsey's decision in retaining Geoff Hurst as a striker in his concrete 4–3–3 formation was thoroughly justified—although it cost some fraying nerves around the stadium before the match was won. The West Germans bit hard at the England team in the early stages with the rotund Hamburg centre forward, Seeler,

winning balls in the air he should not have done. Held and Haller battered continually against the English defences, and Haller put West Germany ahead twelve minutes after the elegant Wilson made one of his rare mistakes in the competition by feebly heading the ball down towards his feet.

England came forward again and Stiles, Peters, Moore and Bobby Charlton gained control in midfield. Six minutes later, Moore lobbed a free kick into the West German area and Hurst directed his header fiercely into the corner of Tilkowski's net.

In the second half, England stayed firmly in control but their opponents' defence held, until twelve minutes from time Peters scored from a deflection. There now seemed little hope for West Germany, but once again their reluctance to surrender proved costly for England. In the last seconds after Jack Charlton had given away a free kick on the edge of the penalty area, the England goal fell; Weber forced the ball through, past Banks, from close range.

And so in to extra time: but here England proved themselves infinitely fitter and better equipped for the extra half-hour. The young Alan Ball was especially busy, his legs tirelessly running over the soggy grass. It was Ball who set up the move from which Hurst shot the ball against the West German crossbar; it bounced down and the Russian referee, after consulting a linesman, gave a goal. A reasonable doubt still exists about the goal's validity. But there was no doubt about Hurst's third goal with the last kick of the game which rocketed into the West German net. Alf Ramsey's side certainly deserved their win.

England—Banks, Cohen, Wilson, Stiles, J. Charlton, Moore, Ball, Hurst, R. Charlton, Hunt, Peters.

West Germany—Tilkowski, Hottges, Schulz, Weber, Schnellinger, Beckenbauer, Haller, Seeler, Held, Overath, Emmerich.

Celtic 2 Internazionale, Milan 1—European Cup Final, 25 May 1967, National Stadium, Lisbon

A famous occasion in British football: after years in which clubs like Real Madrid, Benfica and Inter-Milan had been the dominating powers in Europe's premier cup competition, the balance of power shifted for the first time to a club on the other side of the North Sea.

It was to Celtic, renowned for their refreshing attacking skills, that the honour finally fell and what made their victory yet more satisfying was the way they broke down the deadening *catenaccio* defensive tactics employed by the Milan team, who with them had won the trophy in 1964 and 1965.

When Celtic arrived with thousands of their merry supporters in Lisbon, they had already won the Scottish League Championship, the Scottish Cup, the Scottish League Cup and knocked out Dukla Prague in the European Cup semi-final. Their confidence

Facchetti of Inter-Milan deflects a shot
from Bobby Lennox of Celtic in the 1967
European Cup Final

was naturally at boiling point but the Inter-Milan side they were to face had only been beaten once in European competition in four years, and would provide their most difficult challenge. But Inter-Milan were handicapped by the absence of the injured Spanish midfield tactician, Suarez, and their Brazilian right winger, Jair.

Inter-Milan's tactics of claiming an early goal and then shutting up their own fortress for the duration was initially successful: Craig brought down Cappellini after seven minutes and Mazzola scored from the penalty. Celtic was now faced with the task of finding the fortress key, and for a long frustrating period it eluded them.

But Celtic kept moving forward in attacking waves with left back Tommy Gemmell adding full power to the seige. Jimmy Johnstone weaved and meandered, but the Inter-Milan defence continued to hold out beyond half-time. Sarti, in the Inter-Milan goal, sprang about his goal line like a black panther, and when two shots by Auld and Gemmell did beat him the posts were there

Below: Celtic supporters are jubilant after Celtic has beaten Inter-Milan 2—1 in the 1967 European Cup Final. Right: An outstanding team: Alex James leads out Arsenal in their heyday in the 1930s. Second comes Eddie Hapgood, who himself captained England

to throw the ball out of his goal. Sarti was finally beaten by Gemmell with a savage shot from Craig's pass for the equalizer. The Celtic fans howled their delight and, when five minutes from time Chalmers deflected a shot from Murdoch into Sarti's net, the Inter-Milan players lowered their shoulders knowing the game was lost. When the referee blew his whistle, the pitch suddenly overflowed with bellowing Celtic supporters in kilts and baggy trousers, shirt tails flapping round their knees. Celtic went home in triumph—it was an achievement which they would surely rarely better.

Celtic—Simpson, Craig, Gemmell, Murdoch, McNeil, Clark, Johnstone, Wallace, Chalmers, Auld, Lennox.

Inter-Milan—Sarti, Picchi, Burgnich, Guarneri, Facchetti, Bedin, Corso, Bicicli, Mazzola, Cappelini, Domenghini.

8 SOME FAMOUS FOOTBALL CLUBS

Ajax Amsterdam

Emerged as Europe's most successful club side in the early 1970s. Won the European Cup in three successive seasons—in 1971, by 2—0 against the Greek side Panathinaikos at Wembley; in 1972, by 2—0 against Inter-Milan at Rotterdam; and in 1973, by 1—0 against Juventus of Turin in Belgrade. They owed their astonishing upsurge to two inspired managers, first to the tough sergeant-major, Rinus Michels, who built up the side in the mid-sixties, and later the chatty Rumanian, Stefan Kovacs. The club also had an immensely gifted footballer in Johan Cruyff to build the side around.

In recent seasons Ajax have shared domination of their own domestic league with Feyenoord of Rotterdam. Ajax were founded in 1900 and became a major club after professionalism was introduced in Holland in 1953. In 1957–58, they reached the quarter finals of the European Cup and the final in 1969 when they lost 1—4 to A.C. Milan. Since Cruyff's transfer to Barcelona for nearly a million pounds sterling, the club showed signs of decline after being knocked out of the European Cup in 1973–74 season by C.S. Sofia. But they still have some brilliant players in Keizer, Krol and the young Rep.

Arsenal

Built up a reputation as one of the world's most outstanding club sides between the two world wars when they had a sensational run of successes in the Football League and F.A. Cup. Arsenal's finest era was under Herbert Chapman, a superb manager, who took control in 1925. It was under his guidance that Arsenal won the League championship altogether five times in the thirties and the F.A. Cup in 1930 and 1936. Before he died in 1934, Chapman brought some splendid players to Highbury including Alex James, David Jack, Eddie Hapgood, Ted Drake and Cliff Bastin. Arsenal were one of the first top professional sides to go on foreign tours and their nickname 'The Gunners' became famous overseas. After the war, they had to build up a new combination but were soon winning cups again.

They won the League championship in 1947–48 and 1952–53, and the F.A. Cup under Joe Mercer's captaincy in 1950. Then for several years, after losing their older players like Leslie Compton, Mercer, with a broken leg, and Wally Barnes, they went into decline. But after Bertie Mee took over as manager from Billy Wright in the mid-1960s, another formidable, if slightly unattractive side, emerged.

Arsenal won the Inter-Fairs Cup in 1970 and a year later became only the second side of this century to win the Football Championship and the F.A. Cup in the same season. Charlie George scored Arsenal's winning goal in the final at Wembley against Liverpool. Arsenal were originally founded in 1886 by a group of munition

Left: A natural goalscorer, Jimmy Greaves in his Chelsea days shoots for goal against Tottenham, whom he later joined. Right: Cliff Jones of Tottenham and Wales was a member of the Tottenham team that achieved the double in 1960–61

workers at Woolwich and named Royal Arsenal F.C. Later the name was changed to Woolwich Arsenal, and finally to Arsenal in 1914. The club moved to its present headquarters at Highbury in North London in 1913.

C. F. Barcelona
One of the world's wealthiest clubs, happy and able recently to pay out nearly a million pounds on signing the Dutch wizard Johan Cruyff. The transfer was completely justified because Cruyff's new membership attracted attendances of 80,000 spectators paying high prices, and the club were soon well on the way to making a profit from the deal, as well as being able to extend their ground capacity at Nuevo Campo to 115,000 spectators. Barcelona have always had a great rivalry with Real Madrid but have a far poorer record in European competition than the proud champions from the Spanish capital. In the 1960–61 season they did manage to reach the final of the European Cup but lost 3–2 to Benfica.

Barcelona have relied on some outstanding foreign players in their team, including the Hungarian, Sandor Kocsis, a lethal kangaroo-necked header of the ball who came to Spain following the Hungarian revolution in 1956, and another Hungarian, Ladislav Kubla, an inside forward with the frenzied dynamism of a gypsy orchestra. One of their forwards in the late fifties was Luis Suarez, born in Corunna. When in possession he could almost make the ball disappear from the opposition's view. He was transferred to Inter-Milan for £150,000 in 1961. Barcelona were founded in 1899 by a naturalized Swiss, Don Juan Gamper.

Members of the 'Busby Babes' Manchester United team tragically killed in the 1958 air crash at Munich: captain Roger Byrne and the out- standing Duncan Edwards in action against Aston Villa in the 1957 Cup Final. Inset: Sir Matt Busby in his playing days for Manchester City

Benfica

One of the imperial sides of post-war European soccer. Their modern rise stemmed from the appointment of that brilliant Hungarian manager, Bella Guttman, who played for his own Olympic team in 1921–24 as a half back. Guttman's ubiquitous career had already spanned a long era in his own country and in Holland, Italy and South America before his arrival at the Estadio da Luz in 1958. In 1961 under his command, Benfica defeated C. F. Barcelona 3—2, in a fluctuating European Cup final; and a year later they beat Real Madrid 5—2 in Amsterdam to retain the trophy. This must have been one of the most exciting matches in history, and at one stage Benfica, at 1—3 down, were all but paralyzed. But Guttman had introduced a new discovery into his team—a young black bomber called 'Eusebio' Ferreira da Silva from Mozambique. Eusebio scored three goals in the second half to cap three by Puskas for Real Madrid, and promptly established his name as a world-class striker.

Benfica took part in the World Club Cup Final in 1961 and 1962 against Penarol of Uruguay and Santos of Brazil, but lost on both occasions. Guttman left but Benfica continued to be a serious force, assisted often by Eusebio's violent shooting and the calm efficient mid-field work of another former resident of Mozambique, Mario Coluña. Benfica were finalists again in the European Cup Final in 1963, and again in 1965 and 1968. They were originally founded in 1904 by a young football fanatic from Lisbon called Cosmé Damiao. Membership was restricted to players from the Portuguese empire. Benfica won their first Portuguese Champion-ship, which had been started in 1934, in the 1935–36 season.

Celtic

The wearers of the green and white hoops have been a dominating force in Scottish football since their foundation in 1888 by a group of Irish Catholics in Glasgow's East End. Only their great rivals Glasgow Rangers have enjoyed such a flowing run of success in the Scottish League, the Scottish Cup and the Scottish League Cup. There has always been an intense rivalry between the two clubs and their confrontations have sometimes produced an almost holy war on the terraces of Parkhead and Ibrox Park between the Celtic 'papists' and the Rangers 'protestants'. Celtic have been the stronger side of late, and their surprising but highly popular victory in the European Cup Final in Lisbon in 1967 against Inter-Milan (see Famous Matches) was the most memor-able achievement in their history. Their head pilot in recent seasons has been Jock Stein—captain of Celtic when they won the Scottish League and Cup double in 1954 and now a manager of great renown.

Celtic had a remarkable run of success in nine seasons from 1965–1974 winning nine Scottish Championships, five Cup Finals

and five League Cups. They reached the European Cup Final
again in 1970 but lost to the Dutch side, Feyenoord. They have
paraded some legendary players in their time, including an Irishman, Patsy Gallagher, known as the 'mighty atom' who left Celtic
after a tremendous era in 1926, Jimmy McMenemy, a pre-First
World War constructive player of great distinction, Jimmy
McGrory, a native of Glasgow, who scored a record 410 Scottish
League goals between 1922 and 1938, and in more modern times
Charlie Tully (another Irishman), Bobby Evans, Tommy Gemmell
and Jimmy Johnstone.

Chelsea

A club founded in an area of West London more famous for its
artists and resident bohemians than its footballers. Since 1905,
when the 'blues' first started playing league football at Stamford
Bridge, off the Fulham Road, they often earned a reputation for
eccentricity through fickleness in combat. In the twenties and
thirties, they became known as 'the great unpredictables' and in
the music hall 'the pensioners'. Chelsea tended to run around a
lot and win nothing until the 1954–55 season, when they won the
Football League Championship for the first and only time in their
history. Ted Drake, the old Arsenal player, had taken over as
manager, and the side took a great bound forward. They owed
much to the goal-scoring powers of their captain, Roy Bentley, a
ubiquitous centre forward. Chelsea went down into the Second
Division in 1962 but were promoted again a year later. Under
Tommy Docherty's management, a strong, youthful side was
established but again a certain hesitancy assailed them at the
supreme hour.

Chelsea lost two F.A. Cup semi-finals in 1965 and 1966, when
they were expected to win, and when they did reach Wembley in
1967 against Spurs, they put on a pathetic display and deservedly
lost by 2—1. Jimmy Greaves, whom Chelsea launched on a
spectacular goal-scoring career back in the late fifties, played
against them. But good things were to come. When Dave Sexton
took over as manager from Tommy Docherty, Chelsea re-
organized themselves and reached the Cup Final in 1970 against
Leeds. This proved a remarkable double affair involving skill and
brawn which went to a replay after a 2—2 draw at Wembley. In
the replay at Old Trafford Leeds looked in total command, and led
by a goal from Mick Jones until late in the game; but a shrewd
pass by Charlie Cooke gave Peter Osgood an equalizer. In extra
time Dave Webb headed the winning goal for Chelsea. A year
later Chelsea won the European Cup Winners Cup, beating Real
Madrid in a replay in Athens. The old music-hall image had been
banished—at least for a time. Stamford Bridge is now under
reconstruction costing well over £1 million.

Feyenoord
The Rotterdam club founded in 1908 by the mining tycoon C. R. J. Kieboom developed into one of the strongest Dutch teams and were the first side to bring the European Cup to Holland when they beat Celtic 2—1 in the final in Milan. Their magnificent victory, which their Swedish centre forward Ove Kindvall capped with a winning goal in extra time, was followed by victory over the Argentine club Estudiantes in a rough and tumble in the World Club Championship. In the following seasons, Ajax of Amsterdam took over as the dominating force in the European Cup but Feyenoord had paved the way. One of their best seasons in Dutch football was in 1968–69 when they won the League and Cup. One of their finest players before the Second World War was Puck van Heel, who won sixty-four Dutch caps as a left half.

Honved
One of the legendary post-war Hungarian teams who in the early fifties could claim the services of Ferenc Puskas, Josef Bozsik, goalkeeper Gyuala Grocis and Zoltan Czibor. Their much-vaunted team travelled to England in 1954 shortly after Hungary had mauled England on two occasions. Wolves played them in a friendly match and won a really exciting game by 3—2. The Honved side broke up after the Hungarian revolution, and their most famous player Puskas went to Real Madrid. The side was founded in 1949 as a military club, managed by the brilliant manager Gustav Sebes (who also ran the national team), and won the League five out of seven times in their first seasons. But after Puskas and others left things were never quite the same again, although Honved did win the Cup in 1964.

Leeds United
The Yorkshire club were founded in 1920 but did not really make an impact as a class team until the 1960s, when a new manager, Don Revie, rescued them from near-oblivion. Revie, a former Manchester City and England international, built up a fine side

around such players as centre half Jack Charlton, Billy Bremner, Norman Hunter and Johnny Giles. Leeds were promoted from the Second Division in 1964 and just missed winning the Football League Championship a year later. They also reached the F.A. Cup Final in the season, losing 2—1 to Liverpool. Since then they have rarely not been competing for the honours and have had as many disappointments as triumphs. In 1962 they won the F.A. Cup, the Football League Championship in 1969, and the European Fairs Cup twice, in 1968 and 1971.

In 1970, they were in the running for the grand slam, but finally missed winning the Football League, lost to Chelsea in the F.A. Cup final replay and were beaten by Celtic in the European Cup semi-finals. Don Revie's team have often been criticized for their rough tactics and blatant gamesmanship. But after the Football Association had given them a £3,000 suspended fine for their misconduct in 1973, Leeds entered the next season with a new friendly spirit. Their play became also of a remarkably high standard, inspired by a far more diplomatic Billy Bremner. Leeds broke an old record set by Liverpool in 1949 of playing nineteen League matches without defeat, winning the Championship.

Internazionale, Milan
Two victories in the 1964 and 1965 European Cup Finals against Real Madrid in Vienna and Benfica in their own stadium, San Siro, put Inter-Milan on the throne of European soccer. Their manager, Helenio Herrera, Argentinian-born and French-nationalized, had instigated a rigorous tactical plan. This was to stay back in defence and hope for a goal when the other side were looking the other way. His system was called *catenaccio* and while often being totally boring to watch, was not only highly frustrating to the opposition but also effective in gaining favourable results.

Inter-Milan had been founded in 1908 by breakaway members of Inter's great rivals A.C. Milan, and won the Italian League for the first time in 1910. Under Herrera, they won the Italian Championship three times in 1963, 1965 and 1966. Inter were successful in both their championship finals in 1964 and 1965, in each case against Independiente of Buenos Aires.

Herrera left Inter-Milan in 1968 after a bold, attacking Celtic had beaten his dour side a season before by 2—1 in another European Cup Final in Lisbon. The side began to break up but only briefly. In 1972, they reached the European Cup Final again before being beaten 2—1 by Ajax of Amsterdam in Rotterdam.

Liverpool
A side formidably hard to beat on their own ground at Anfield. The raucous and almost fanatical chanting from the 'Kop' end of the ground by thousands of singing supporters have often provided Liverpool with a twelfth man in critical games. The Club

have always had an intense rivalry with Everton down the road at Goodison Park. The matches between the Liverpool reds and the Everton blues always create an almost religious fervour in the city for weeks beforehand, and defeat can shatter morale.

Liverpool were founded in 1892 and won their first First Division Championship in the 1900–1901 season. Their most outstanding team was the post-Second World War combination built up during the 1960s by the granite-faced Scottish manager, Bill Shankly. Liverpool were promoted again to the First Division in 1962 under his command and with fine players like Hunt, Thompson, Yeats and St John in the side, they went on to win two League Championships and the F.A. Cup before the end of 1966. In 1965–66, they equalled Arsenal's record of winning the championship seven times. Liverpool, with a side changed through time and with the addition of talented players like Heighway and Keegan, won the Football League Championship in 1972–73 and the F.A. Cup in 1974. Shankly was still in command. But disappointment hung heavily in 1974 when Red Star of Yugoslavia eliminated Liverpool from the European Cup. Liverpool have so far failed to achieve anything notable in Europe. In the 1966 European Cup Winners Cup Final at Hampden Park, they were defeated 2—1 by Borussia Dortmund.

Manchester United

This is England's most popular post-war club. The Red Devils had three decisive eras after Sir Matt Busby took over as manager at the end of the war. His first team, captained by John Carey, won the F.A. Cup in 1948 in an epic match against Blackpool. When this side broke up at the beginning of the fifties, Busby brought some young players into the team, amongst them Duncan Edwards and Roger Byrne. They became known as the 'Busby Babes' and created an astonishing reputation for the exciting quality of their play. The side were on their way back from playing a European Cup tie in Belgrade when their plane crashed on take-off at Munich airport. Eight players were killed—Byrne, Bent, Colman, Jones, Pegg, Taylor, Wheelan, and Edwards, who died in hospital later. Busby was badly injured in the crash but survived to build up yet another masterly team.

The sixties side included Denis Law, Bobby Charlton and that enigmatic genius, George Best. This team gave Busby his greatest reward when they won the European Cup at Wembley in 1968, beating Benfica 4—1 after extra time. Since then Busby has retired as manager and United went into decline. Charlton retired, Best disappeared from football, came back and disappeared again, while Law went over the road to Manchester City. At the end of the 1973–74 season United were relegated to the Second Division. What those three United teams gave was the very best— and their achievements will never be forgotten.

Few games have attracted such fascination as the Chelsea–Moscow Dynamo match at Chelsea in 1945. Over 80,000 spectators attended and at least 10,000 gatecrashers. Here the Russian goalkeeper Khomich makes a startling save

Milan AC
First Italian club to win the European Cup when they beat Benfica 2—1 at Wembley in 1963. The Brazilian Altafini scored both the goals for Milan and the man who put him through was the young Gianni Rivera who subsequently established himself as one of Italy's finest tacticians. Milan won another prize under his direction at the end of the 1972–73 season when they won the European Cup Winners Cup, beating Leeds. Milan were originally founded in 1899 as the Milan Cricket and Football Club which was made up of players from England and Italy. They are now one of the wealthiest clubs in the world and share the huge San Siro stadium with their rivals Internazionale Milan.

Moscow Dynamo
Founded in 1887 by an English textile director called Clement Charnock. His brother Harry took over the club which consisted of players from a local textile mill. In later years they were again taken over, this time by the Soviet Electrical Trades Union and this is how they became known as Dynamo. They became members of the Russian First Division when it was formed in 1936 and topped it on several occasions afterwards. One of their most famous players was Lev Yashin, who played over fifty times for his country in goal after the war. He is now their manager. Another famous Dynamo goalkeeper was 'Tiger' Khomich who was in the side when Moscow Dynamo made their famous tour of Britain in 1945. They beat Cardiff City 10—1, drew 3—3 with Chelsea, beat

Arsenal 4—3 and drew with Glasgow Rangers 2—2. The tour aroused tremendous interest, especially at Chelsea where nearly 90,000 fans gathered to see them, many of them gate-crashers in uniform.

FC Bayern Munich
With national stars like Franz Beckenbauer, Gerd Muller and Paul Breitner in the side, Bayern became the new club kings of Europe after beating Atletico Madrid 4—0 in a European Cup Final replay in 1974. Bayern are strong, rich and successful. But they haven't always been: they were originally left out of the new West German professional league—the Bundesliga—in favour of their then more positive rivals across the city, Munich 1860, when the league was formed in 1963. But they were elected to the league for the 1965–66 season and went on to win the European Cup Winners Cup in 1967 against Glasgow Rangers in Nuremberg by 1—0 after extra time. Bayern are now the wealthiest club in West Germany and owe much to the encouragement of their president and millionaire mason, Wilhelm Neudecker, and a shrewd coach from Yugoslavia, Zlatko Cajkovski. They recently moved their head-quarters to the new Olympic Stadium.

Penarol
Founded in 1891 through British influence as the Cricket and Football Club, Penarol, the aristocrats of Uruguay, many years later became World Club Champions, first in 1961 when they beat Benfica and then five years later when they beat Real Madrid. They have often dominated Uruguayan football, winning the championship over thirty times, twice without losing a match, in 1967 and 1968. They play most of their matches at the Centenary Stadium in Montevideo which they share with another famous Uruguayan club, Nacional.

Real Madrid
The world's outstanding post-war club became virtual rulers of the European Cup after its inception in the mid-fifties, winning it five times in succession from 1956. They were probably at their peak in 1960 when they also won the World Club Championship. Another European Cup was won in 1966 but since then, deprived of such outstanding players as di Stefano, Puskas, Kopa, Del Sol, Santamaria and Rial, and later Gento, their standards have declined. Recently Real signed the West German player Gunter Netzer to try and reclaim their lost prestige but the move was not initially successful.

But memories of the many glorious hours in which Puskas and Di Stefano foxed and teased the opposition at the magnificent Santiago Bernabeau Stadium live on. The most vivid of them all is surely of the night Real beat Eintracht Frankfurt 7—3 (see Famous Matches) at Glasgow in 1960. Real lifted the arts of soccer on to a higher plane of near-perfection that evening. Their deeds were almost uncanny, born of some superior force.

Real was originally founded in 1898 by students playing soccer near the Madrid Bull Ring. But it was officially born in 1902 and given the title 'Royal' by King Alfonso XIII in 1920. But their days of international power were not born until 1943 when Don Santiago Bernabeau took over as president. He was instrumental in the opening of their modern stadium in 1948 and created an almost family atmosphere in its precincts. The playing staff have always trained and played in an atmosphere of great luxury. They are all made to feel like players of great distinction and this was only reflected in their large salaries. Real have always been a club who have cared for their players, especially after their playing days are over.

Perhaps the most important signing Real made was that of Alfredo di Stefano in 1953 from the Millionaires Club in Colombia. He was a football aristocrat who scored arrogant goals. He liked to roam all over the pitch, end to end, and a memory remains of him once dribbling the ball from his own goal line to set up a goal for Puskas at the other end. Real built up the team around him with other expensive foreign talent, notably Ferenc Puskas from Hungary, Hector Rial from Colombia, Raymond Kopa from France and José Santamaria from Nacional in Uruguay. With so many princes at court it was hardly surprising that many, many prizes were won by the men in all white.

Santos

Blessed with such an incomparable player as Pele in their ranks, Santos have never been slow to show off their most prized product around the world during long and financially lucrative tours. They had held a high reputation for playing achievements in Brazil all the way back to their foundation in 1913, which involved a quick move from Santos to their present headquarters in São Paulo. But their finest times came many years later, when young Pele arrived at the club in the 1950s. In 1959, he scored an astonishing 100 goals, and in 1962 and 1963, he helped Santos win the World Club Cup twice in two leg matches against Benfica and A.C. Milan. Pele was at his irresistable best during this era, but Santos also had some other fine players to assist in the operation, including the Brazil goalkeeper Gilmar, Zito in midfield, and Pepe and Coutino in the forward line. In later years, Carlos Alberto, Brazil's captain in the 1970 World Cup Finals, Clqdoaldo and Paulo Cesar came along to boost the team. Pele duly scored his 1000th goal and then threatened to retire at the end of the 1974 season. It was a thought Santos, Brazil and the football world dared not contemplate.

Tottenham Hotspur

For football purists, the two prize-winning Tottenham sides of
1950–51 and 1960–61 are hard to match on the post-war British
front from the points of view of style and lucidity. The first side
managed by Arthur Rowe in 1949 won promotion from the Second
Division and the Football League championship using tactics
known as push-and-run. It was simple but beautiful to watch, and
highly effective. Rowe had the players exploit it to the full. The
team included Alf Ramsey at right back, captain Ron Burgess at
left half, the present manager Bill Nicholson at right half, and that
handsome duet, Eddie Baily and Les Medley, who formed the
left wing. This team broke up towards the mid-fifties and a new
side began to be shaped under the captaincy of Danny Blanchflower, who had been transferred from Aston Villa. When Nicholson became manager, he made three vital signings which helped
bring Tottenham to their peak again towards the end of the decade.
Two were from Scotland, John White, nicknamed 'the ghost', and
Dave Mackay, and Cliff Jones came from Swansea. Their great
year was 1960–61, when Tottenham, or 'Spurs' (their famous
nickname), won the Cup and League double—the first side to
achieve this distinction during this century. A season later,
Tottenham reached the semi-finals of the European Cup but lost
in two exciting legs against Benfica. But they won the 1962 F.A.
Cup against Burnley, one of the goals being scored by a new and
brilliant arrival, Jimmy Greaves. A year later Greaves played a
prominent part in Tottenham's victory against Atletico Madrid in
Rotterdam. Those were the glorious days of the Spurs and they
have never been quite the same although they did win the F.A.
Cup in 1967, the Football League Cup twice and the UEFA Cup in
1972.

Tottenham have always had a reputation for playing attractive
football. Their early beginnings were on Tottenham Marshes in
the 1880s. They took over their famous headquarters at White
Hart Lane in 1899; and their most satisfactory achievement
between the wars was the 1—0 F.A. Cup victory against Wolves in
1921.

Johann Cruyff, Barcelona's £900,000 signing from Ajax of Amsterdam, storms along with the ball

9 WORLD SOCCER ALL STARS

Some football writers find that an ideal cure for insomnia lies in making up lists of ideal football combinations. These two post-war sides representing Great Britain and the Rest of the World would surely have provided one of the most epic matches in history if time had allowed them all to be brought together at the same time to play. Many famous names have been reluctantly left out, like Tommy Lawton (England), Peter Doherty (N. Ireland), Billy Steel (Scotland), Eusebio (Portugal), Sandos Kocsis (Hungary), Josef Masopust (Czechoslovakia) and George Best (N. Ireland).

GREAT BRITAIN
1   Gordon Banks (England)
2   George Young (Scotland)
3   Ray Wilson (England)
4   Danny Blanchflower (Northern Ireland)
5   Billy Wright (England)
6   Duncan Edwards (England)
7   Stanley Matthews (England)
8   Bobby Charlton (England)
9   John Charles (Wales)
10   Denis Law (Scotland)
11   Tom Finney (England)
Substitutes: Jim Baxter (Scotland), Bobby Moore (England), Jimmy Greaves (England); sub-goalkeeper: Frank Swift (England)

REST OF THE WORLD
1   Lev Yashin (Russia)
2   Dejalma Santos (Brazil)
3   Giacinto Facchetti (Italy)
4   Jozsef Bozsik (Hungary)
5   Carlo Parola (Italy)
6   Franz Beckenbauer (West Germany)
7   Garrincha (Brazil)
8   Pele (Brazil)
9   Alfredo di Stefano (Argentina and Spain)
10   Ferenc Puskas (Hungary)
11   Johan Cruyff (Holland)
Substitutes: Luis Suarez (Spain), José Santamaria (Uruguay and Spain), Antonio Rattin (Argentina); sub-goalkeeper: Dino Zoff (Italy).

The result?—that is part of the fascinating argument. But I would guess the Rest would get by with two goals to spare. Or would they?

FURTHER READING

Barrett, Norman (Ed.) *World Soccer From A to Z* (Pan)

Busby, Sir Matt *Soccer at the Top* (Weidenfeld & Nicolson)

Creek, F. N. S. *Soccer* (Teach Yourself Books)

Davies, Hunter *The Glory Game* (Weidenfeld & Nicolson)

Glanville, Brian *Goalkeepers are Different* (Puffin)

Glanville, Brian *The Sunday Times History of the World Cup* (Thompson Newspapers Ltd.)

Green, Geoffrey *Great Moments in Sport: Soccer* (Pelham)

Hopcraft, Arthur *The Football Man* (Collins; Penguin)

James, Brian *England v Scotland* (Pelham)

Miller, David *World Cup 1970* (Heinemann)

Moynihan, John *Football Fever* (Quartet)

Moynihan, John *Park Football* (Pelham)

Parkinson, M. and Hall, W. (Eds) *Football Report* (Pelham)

Sewell, Albert *The Observer's Book of Association Football* (Warne)

GLOSSARY

Angle Intersection of goal post and crossbar

Back-pass A pass by a player to his goalkeeper

Banana kick Swerving shot struck with the outside of the foot to achieve a side-spin effect. Often used in free-kick situations to bypass a defensive wall

Cross Pass from a player on the wing into the goalmouth; can be in the air or on the ground

Chip Delicate kick which enables a player to lift the ball over an opponent's head by way of a short, sharp jab

Dropped ball Method of restarting the game after the referee has stopped play (eg: to attend to an injured player). The referee drops the ball between two opposing players who may then play it after it has touched the ground

Equalizer Goal which brings the scores of both teams level

Handball An offence where a player (apart from either goalkeeper) touches the ball with his hand or any part of his arm below the shoulder

Kill ball Stop the ball dead by bringing it under control with one movement

Linkman A player who provides a link between the defenders and the forwards

Linesman Official running along the touchline with a flag to assist the referee in the running of the game. He signals when the ball goes out of play and when a player is offside

Mark Watch and follow an opponent to prevent him receiving the ball

Offside When there are no defenders between an attacker and the goal, apart from the goalkeeper

Overlap Action of a full-back or other defensive player running into a position normally adopted by the winger, to add strength to an attack

Penalty Direct free-kick from a spot twelve yards from the goal, following a foul or handball inside the penalty area by a defender. No defenders are allowed to stand between the spot and the goal when the kick is taken

Striker Attacking player whose sole job is to score goals. In today's game there are generally two, three or four strikers in a team, depending on the tactics

Sweeper Defensive player whose job is to deal with any loose balls which get past the defenders

Scout A talent-spotter who tours football grounds in search of good players for his club

Sliding tackle Method of taking the ball from an opponent by sliding along the ground with one leg outstretched

Tactics System of play (defensive, attacking, etc.) usually changes from match to match. For example a team playing at home would have three or four forwards, but playing away might have only one or two

Through-pass Pass played straight forward to an attacker as opposed to a square or diagonal pass

Wall Line-up of defenders between the goal and the place from where a free-kick is being taken, to prevent the kicker shooting straight at the goal. The wall must be at least ten yards from the ball

INDEX

Illustration references in italic